Contents

LINQ for Visual C# 2008

by Fabio Claudio Ferracchiati

Over the past 20 years object-oriented programming languages have evolved to become the premier tools for enterprise application development. They've been augmented by frameworks, APIs, and rapid application-development tools. Yet what's been missing is a way to intimately tie object-oriented programs to relational databases (and other data that doesn't exist as objects). The object paradigm is conceptually different from the relational one and this creates significant impedance between the objects programs use and the tables where data resides. ADO.NET provides a convenient interface to relational data, but not an object-oriented one. For example, this pseudocode would be really cool:

```
// A class representing a table of employees
Employees e = new Employees();

// Set the row identifier to one
e.ID = 1;

// Retrieve the row where ID=1
e.Retrieve();

// Change the Name column value to Alan
e.Name = "Alan";

// Modify the database data
e.Upate();
```

The pseudocode shows an object-oriented approach to data management; no query or SQL statement is visible to developers. You need to think about only what you have to do, not how to do it. This approach to combining object-oriented and relational technologies has been called the Object-Relational Mapping (ORM) model.

Although Microsoft has embedded ORM capabilities in its Dynamics CRM 3.0 application server and should soon do the same in ADO.NET 3.0, it doesn't yet provide this programming model to .NET developers. To run a simple SQL query, ADO.NET programmers have to store the SQL in a Command object, associate the Command with a Connection object and execute it on that Connection object, then use a DataReader or other object to retrieve the result set. For example, the following code is necessary to retrieve the single row accessed in the pseudocode presented earlier.

```
// Specify the connection to the DB
SqlConnection c = new SqlConnection(…);

// Open the connection
c.Open();


// Specify the SQL Command
SqlCommand cmd = new SqlCommand(@"
    SELECT
        *
    FROM
        Employees e
    WHERE
        e.ID = @p0
");

// Add a value to the parameter
cmd.Parameters.AddWithValue("@p0", 1);

// Excute the command
DataReader dr = c.Execute(cmd);

// Retrieve the Name column value
while (dr.Read()) {
    string name = dr.GetString(0);
}

// Update record using another Command object
…

// Close the connection
c.Close();
```

Not only is this a lot more code than the ORM code, but there's also no way for the C# compiler to check our query against our use of the data it returns. When we retrieve the employee's name we have to know the column's position in the database table to find it in the result. It's a common mistake to retrieve the wrong column and get a type exception or bad data at run time.

ADO.NET moved toward ORM with strongly typed `DataSets`. But we still have to write the same kind of code, using a DataAdapter instead of a Command object. The DataAdapter contains four Command objects, one for each database operation—`SELECT`, `DELETE`, `INSERT`, and `UPDATE`—and we have fill the correct one with the appropriate SQL code.

.NET can also handle XML and nonrelational data sources, but then we have to know other ways to query information, such as XPath or XQuery. SQL and XML can be made to work together but only by shifting mental gears at the right time.

What Is LINQ?

At the Microsoft Professional Developers Conference (PDC) 2005, Anders Hejlsberg and his team presented a new approach, Language Integrated Query (LINQ), which unifies the way data can be retrieved in .NET. LINQ provides a uniform way to retrieve data from any object that implements the `IEnumerable<T>` interface. With LINQ, arrays, collections, relational data, and XML are all potential data sources.

Why LINQ?

With LINQ, you can use the same syntax to retrieve data from any data source:

```
var query = from e in employees
where e.id == 1
select e.name
```

This is not pseudocode; this is LINQ syntax, and it's very similar to SQL. The LINQ team's goal was not to add yet another way to access data, but to provide a native, integrated set of instructions to query any kind of data source. Using C# keywords, we can write data access code as part of C#, and the C# compiler will be able to enforce type safety and even logical consistency. LINQ provides a rich set of instructions to implement complex queries that support data aggregation, joins, sorting, and much more.

Figure 1 presents an overview of LINQ functionality. The top level shows the languages that provide native support for LINQ. Currently, only C# 3.0 and Visual Basic 9.0 offer complete support for LINQ.

The middle level represents the three main parts of the LINQ project:

LINQ to Objects is an API that provides methods that represent a set of *standard query operators* (SQOs) to retrieve data from any object whose class implements the `IEnumerable<T>` interface. These queries are performed against in-memory data.

LINQ to ADO.NET augments SQOs to work against relational data. It is composed of three parts (which appear at the bottom level of Figure 1): **LINQ to SQL** (formerly DLinq) is use to query relational databases such as Microsoft SQL Server. **LINQ to DataSet** supports queries by using ADO.NET data sets and data tables. **LINQ to Entities** is a Microsoft ORM solution, allowing developers to use Entities (an ADO.NET 3.0 feature) to declaratively specify the structure of business objects and use LINQ to query them.

LINQ to XML (formerly XLinq) not only augments SQOs but also includes a host of XML-specific features for XML document creation and queries.

Figure 1. Data domains in which LINQ adds functionality

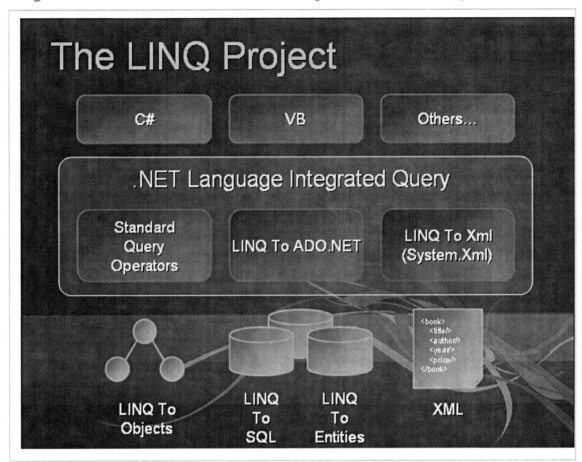

Note   I don't cover LINQ to Entities because the ADO.NET Entity Framework is an ADO.NET 3.0 feature, and is not yet as mature as other technologies that can be used with LINQ.

Now let's see what you need to work with LINQ.

What You Need to Use LINQ

LINQ is a combination of extensions to .NET languages and class libraries that support them. To use it, you'll need the following:

- Obviously LINQ, which is available from the new Microsoft .NET Framework 3.5 that you can download at `http://go.microsoft.com/?linkid=7755937`.

- You can speed up your application development time with LINQ using Visual Studio 2008, which offers visual tools such as LINQ to SQL designer and the Intellisense support with LINQ's syntax. You can obtain a 90-day trial version of Visual Studio 2008 at `http://msdn2.microsoft.com/en-us/vstudio/products/aa700831.aspx`.

- Optionally, you can download the Visual C# 2008 Expression Edition tool at `www.microsoft.com/vstudio/express/download`. It is the free edition of Visual Studio 2008 and offers a lot of LINQ support such as Intellisense and LINQ to SQL designer. To use LINQ to ADO.NET, you need SQL Server 2005, SQL Server 2005 Express Edition, or SQL Server 2000.

Resources

There's a lot of good material available about LINQ:

- The main LINQ Project site (`http://msdn2.microsoft.com/en-us/netframework/aa904594.aspx`) includes a Forums section where thousands of developers discuss LINQ, ask for support, and report bugs.

- From my site (`www.ferracchiati.com`) you can find a lot of useful links for LINQ stuff.

- At `http://shop.ecompanystore.com/mseventdvd/MSD_Shop.asp` you can order the DVD that contains full sessions from PDC 2005, where LINQ was unveiled.

- On the Channel 9 site (`http://channel9.msdn.com`), Anders Hejlsberg and his team are often interviewed about LINQ issues and development.

What's Next?

This book contains three chapters, each dedicated to one of the main aspects of LINQ. The content assumes you're comfortable with C# generics, delegates, and anonymous methods. You can learn and use LINQ without a deep understanding of these topics, but the more you know about them the faster you'll grasp LINQ's concepts and implementation.

Chapter 1 discusses LINQ to Objects, with a sample program that illustrates its major functionality.

Chapter 2 provides a complete description of LINQ to SQL (LINQ's components for accessing relational data) and its great functionalities. A rich sample program demonstrates its features.

Chapter 3 covers LINQ to XML (LINQ's components for accessing XML data). You'll see how to generate XML from queries and interrogate XML documents to retrieve data by using LINQ syntax.

Chapter 1: LINQ to Objects

In this chapter we'll study LINQ fundamentals by exploring its features for querying in-memory objects. We'll start with some simple examples to get an idea of what programming with LINQ to Objects involves, then we'll look at examples for all of LINQ's standard query operators.

Introduction

Data domains are different from object domains. When we deal with objects like arrays and collections, we use iteration to retrieve their elements. If we're looking for a particular element based on its content rather than its index, we have to use a loop and process each element individually. For example, for an array of strings there is no built-in method to retrieve all elements whose length is equal to a particular value.

LINQ addresses this challenge by providing a uniform way to access data from any data source using familiar syntax. It lets us focus on working with data rather than on accessing it.

LINQ to Objects can be used with any class that implements the `IEnumerable<T>` interface. Let's look at how it works.

A Simple C# 3.0 LINQ to Objects Program

Listing 1-1 is a console program snippet that uses LINQ to Objects to display a specific element in an array.

Listing 1-1. Using LINQ to Objects with List<T>

```
List<Person> people = new List<Person> {
    new Person() { ID = 1,
                IDRole = 1,
                LastName = "Anderson",
                FirstName = "Brad"},
```

```
new Person() { ID = 2,
             IDRole = 2,
             LastName = "Gray",
             FirstName = "Tom"}
    };

    var query = from p in people
                where p.ID == 1
                select new { p.FirstName, p.LastName };

    ObjectDumper.Write(query);
```

In Listing 1-1 you define a collection of Person objects and insert a couple
of elements. List<T> is a generic class that implements IEnumerable<T>, so
it's suitable for LINQ querying.

Next you declare a variable, query, to hold the result of a LINQ query.
Don't worry about the var keyword right now; it will be discussed later in
this chapter, in "Implicitly Typed Local Variables."

You initialize query to a LINQ's *query expression*. The from clause
specifies a data source. The variable p represents an object in the people
collection. The where clause specifies a condition for selecting from the
data source. You want to retrieve just the person whose ID equals 1, so you
specify a Boolean expression, p.ID == 1. Finally, the select clause
specifies what Person data you're interested in retrieving.

The ObjectDumper class is a convenient utility for producing formatted
output. It has only one method, Write(), which has three overloads. (Both
the ObjectDumper.cs source code and the ObjectDumper.dll assembly come
with the book's source code download.)

When you run the program you'll see the result in Figure 1-1.

Figure 1-1. Using LINQ to query a list

This very simple example uses new features from C# 3.0. The first is a query expression that is similar to the one used in SQL and allows developers to use query language syntax that they are already accustomed to. When the compiler finds a query expression in the code, it transforms that expression into C# method calls. Listing 1-2 shows how the query expression in Listing 1-1 would be transformed.

Listing 1-2. Transformed LINQ to Object Code

```
var query = people
            .Where(p => p.ID == 1)
            .Select(p => new { p.FirstName, p.LastName } );
```

The `from` keyword has been removed, leaving just the collection, `people`, against which to perform the query. The `where` and `select` clauses are transformed into two method calls: `Where<T>()` and `Select<T>()`, respectively. They have been concatenated so that the `Where` method's result is filtered by the `Select` method.

You may wonder how this is possible. C# 2.0 doesn't provide these methods for the `List<T>` class or the new C# 3.0 version. C# 3.0 doesn't add these new methods to every class in .NET Framework 3.5. The answer is a new C# 3.0 feature called *extension methods*.

Extension Methods

As the name implies, extension methods extend existing .NET types with new methods. For example, by using extension methods with a `string`, it's possible to add a new method that converts every space in a `string` to an underscore. Listing 1-3 provides an example of an extension method.

Listing 1-3. An Extension Method

```csharp
public static string SpaceToUnderscore(this string source)
{
    char[] cArray = source.ToCharArray();
    string result = null;

    foreach (char c in cArray)
    {
        if (Char.IsWhiteSpace(c))
            result += "_";
        else
            result += c;
    }

    return result;
}
```

Here you define an extension method, `SpaceToUnderscore()`. To specify an extension method you insert the keyword `this` before the first method parameter, which indicates to the compiler the type you want to extend. Note that the method and its class must be `static`. You can use `SpaceToUnderscore()` just like any other `string` method.

Figure 1-2 shows the result of executing this method.

Figure 1-2. Calling an extension method

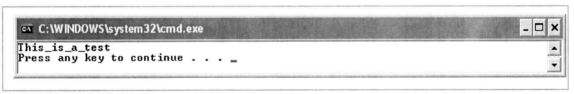

The `Where<T>` and `Select<T>` methods, that the `where` and `select` clauses are transformed into are extension methods defined for the `IEnumerable<T>` interface. They are in the `System.Linq` namespace.

Simply by adding the new `System.Linq` namespace, you can use LINQ with any type that implements `IEnumerable<T>`. You don't have to install a new version of .NET or replace any existing assemblies. You do have to consider a couple of things when implementing and using extension methods, however:

- If you have an extension method and an instance method with the same signature, priority is given to the instance method.

- Properties, events, and operators are not extendable.

Lambda Expressions

Another new C# 3.0 feature is lambda expressions. This feature simplifies coding delegates and anonymous methods.

The argument to the Where<T> method we saw above is an example of a lambda expression:

```
Where(p => p.ID == 1)
```

Lambda expressions allow us to write functions that can be passed as arguments to methods, for example, to supply predicates for subsequent evaluation.

You could use code like that in Listing 1-4 to obtain the same result, but the lambda expression syntax is simpler.

Listing 1-4. Alternative to Lambda Expression Syntax

```
Func<Person, bool> filter = delegate(Person p) { return p.ID == 1; };
var query = people
        .Where(filter)
        .Select(p => new { p.FirstName, p.LastName } );

ObjectDumper.Write(query);
```

Another advantage of lambda expressions is that they give you the ability to perform expression analysis using expression trees.

Expression Trees

LINQ can treat lambda expressions as data at run time. The type Expression<T> represents an expression tree that can be evaluated and changed at run time. It is an in-memory hierarchical data representation where each tree node is part of the entire query expression. There will be nodes representing the conditions, the left and right part of the expression, and so on.

Expression trees make it possible to customize the way LINQ works when it builds queries. For example, a database provider not supported natively by LINQ could provide libraries to translate LINQ expression trees into database queries.

Listing 1-5 shows how to represent a lambda expression with an expression tree.

Listing 1-5. Using an Expression Tree

```
Expression<Func<Person, bool>> e = p => p.ID == 1;

BinaryExpression     body  = (BinaryExpression)e.Body;
MemberExpression     left  = (MemberExpression)body.Left;
ConstantExpression   right = (ConstantExpression)body.Right;

Console.WriteLine(left.ToString());
Console.WriteLine(body.NodeType.ToString());
Console.WriteLine(right.Value.ToString());
```

First you define an Expression<T> variable, e, and assign it the lambda expression you want to evaluate. Then you obtain the "body" of the expression from the Body property of the Expression<T> object. Its Left and Right properties contain the left and right operands of the expression. Depending on the expression, those properties will assume the related type expressed in the formula. In a more complex case you don't know the type to convert to, so you have to use a switch expression to implement any possible case. In our example, to the left there is a member of the

List<Person> type while to the right there is a constant. You cast those properties to the appropriate types.

Figure 1-3 shows the result of running the snippet in Listing 1-5.

Figure 1-3. Displaying a node of an expression tree

The result is clear; the Left property provides the left part of the expression, p.ID. The Right property provides the right part of the expression, 1. Finally, the Body property provides a symbol describing the condition of the expression. In this case EQ stands for *equals*.

Object Initialization Expressions

The code in Listing 1-1 used another C# 3.0 feature called *object initialization expressions*:

```
List<Person> people = new List<Person> {
    new Person() { ID = 1,
                   IDRole = 1,
                   LastName = "Anderson",
                   FirstName = "Brad"},
    new Person() { ID = 2,
                   IDRole = 2,
                   LastName = "Gray",
                   FirstName = "Tom"}
        };
```

Just like an array initializer, an object initialization expression allows us to initialize a new object without calling its constructor and without setting its properties. Let's look at an example in Listing 1-6.

Listing 1-6. Using an Object Initialization Expression

```
// The standard object creation and initialization
Person p1 = new Person();
p1. FirstName = "Brad";
p1.LastName = "Anderson";
ObjectDumper.Write(p1);

// The object initialization expression
Person p2 = new Person { FirstName="Tom", LastName = "Gray" };
ObjectDumper.Write(p2);
```

With object initialization expressions you can create an object directly and set its properties using just one statement. However, you can also write code like in Listing 1-4 *without* specifying the class you are instantiating.

```
.Select(p => new { p.FirstName, p.LastName }
```

It's not an error; it's another new feature called *anonymous types*, and I'll cover it next.

Anonymous Types

In Listing 1-1, note that no type was specified after the new keyword in the object initialization expression. The compiler created a locally scoped anonymous type for us.

Anonymous types let us work with query results on the fly without having to explicitly define classes to represent them. When the compiler encountered

```
select new { p.FirstName, p.LastName };
```

in Listing 1-1 it transparently created a new class with two properties, one for each parameter (see Listing 1-7).

Listing 1-7. A Class for an Anonymous Type

```
internal class ???
{
    private string _firstName;
    private string _lastName;
```

```
    public string FirstName {
        get { return _firstName; }
        set { firstName = value; }
    }
    public string LastName {
        get { return _lastName; }
        set { lastName = value; }
    }
}
```

As you can see in Listing 1-7, the property names are taken directly from the fields specified in the Person class. However, you can indicate the properties for the anonymous type explicitly using the following syntax:

```
new { firstName = p.FirstName, lastName = p.LastName };
```

Now to use the anonymous type in the code you have to respect the new names and the case-sensitive syntax. For example, to print the full name you would use the following:

```
Console.WriteLine("Full Name = {0} {1}", query.firstName, query.lastName);
```

Keep in mind that the anonymous type itself cannot be referenced from the code. How is it possible to access the results of a query if you don't know the name of the new type? The compiler handles this for you by inferring the type. We'll look at this next.

Implicitly Typed Local Variables

A new keyword, var, has been added to C#. When the compiler sees it, it implicitly defines the type of the variable based on the type of expression that initializes the variable. While its use is mandatory with anonymous types, it can be applied even in other cases, such as the following:

- var i = 5; is equivalent to int i = 5;

- var s = "this is a string"; is equivalent to string s = "this is a string";

An implicitly typed local variable must have an initializer. For example, the following declaration is invalid:

```
var s; // wrong definition, no initializer
```

As you can imagine, implicit typing is really useful for complex query results because it eliminates the need to define a custom type for each result.

Note   Implicitly typed local variables cannot be used as method parameters.

Query Evaluation Time

It is important to understand when the query is evaluated at run time. In Listing 1-1 nothing happens in query execution until the ObjectDumper's `Write` method is called. Listing 1-8 looks at the code behind this method:

Listing 1-8. The Core Method of the ObjectDumper Helper Class

```
private void WriteObject(string prefix, object o) {
  if (o == null || o is ValueType || o is string) {
    WriteIndent();
    Write(prefix);
    WriteValue(o);
    WriteLine();
  }
  else if (o is IEnumerable) {
    foreach (object element in (IEnumerable)o) {
      if (element is IEnumerable && !(element is string)) {
        WriteIndent();
        Write(prefix);
        Write("...");
        WriteLine();
        if (level < depth) {
          level++;
          WriteObject(prefix, element);
          level--;
```

```
        }
      }
      else {
        WriteObject(prefix, element);
      }
    }
  }
}
else {
  MemberInfo[] members = null;
  members = o.GetType().GetMembers(BindingFlags.Public |
                                   BindingFlags.Instance);
  WriteIndent();
  Write(prefix);
  bool propWritten = false;
  foreach (MemberInfo m in members) {
    FieldInfo f = m as FieldInfo;
    PropertyInfo p = m as PropertyInfo;
    if (f != null || p != null) {
      if (propWritten) {
        WriteTab();
      }
    else {
      propWritten = true;
    }
    Write(m.Name);
    Write("=");
    Type t = f != null ? f.FieldType : p.PropertyType;
    if (t.IsValueType || t == typeof(string)) {
      WriteValue(f != null ? f.GetValue(o) : p.GetValue(o, null));
    }
    else {
      if (typeof(IEnumerable).IsAssignableFrom(t)) {
        Write("...");
      }
      else {
        Write("{ }");
      }
    }
  }
}
if (propWritten) WriteLine();
  if (level < depth) {
    foreach (MemberInfo m in members) {
```

```
        FieldInfo f = m as FieldInfo;
        PropertyInfo p = m as PropertyInfo;
        if (f != null || p != null) {
          Type t = f != null ? f.FieldType : p.PropertyType;
          if (!(t.IsValueType || t == typeof(string))) {
            object value =
              f != null ? f.GetValue(o) : p.GetValue(o, null);
            if (value != null) {
              level++;
              WriteObject(m.Name + ": ", value);
              level--;
            }
          }
        }
      }
    }
  }
}
```

The Write method makes an internal call to the WriteObject private method
that is the real core of all the ObjectDumper class. In the first section of the
code it checks if the object is null, a string, or an object representing a
value type. In the case of a value type, an output is provided without other
checks. Instead, when the parameter object o implements the
IEnumerable<T> interface the method code goes through each element of the
parameter in order to check if other elements implement IEnumerable<T>. If
not, the object will be passed again to the same method, which will use
.NET Reflection to get its value.

The query expression is evaluated in the foreach statement. This behavior
is guaranteed by the yield keyword used in the methods (called standard
query operators in LINQ; see the next section) defined in the System.Linq
namespace. For an example, let's look at the Where<T> method body in
Listing 1-9:

Listing 1-9. The Body of the Where<T> Method

```
public static IEnumerable<T> Where<T>(
    this IEnumerable<T> source, Func<T, bool> predicate)
{
    if (source == null) throw Error.ArgumentNull("source");
    if (predicate == null)
      throw Error.ArgumentNull("predicate");
    return WhereIterator<T>(source, predicate);
}

static IEnumerable<T> WhereIterator<T>(
    IEnumerable<T> source, Func<T, bool> predicate)
{
    foreach (T element in source) {
        if (predicate(element)) yield return element;
    }
}
```

The Where<T> method calls the private WhereIterator<T> method after having checked that both arguments are not null. (WhereIterator<T> is not called if only one argument is null.) In the WhereIterator<T> method, the yield keyword is used to collect the items that satisfy the condition expressed with the predicate delegate function.

It's possible to cache the result of a query using the ToList and ToArray methods. Let's look at the example in Listing 1-10:

Listing 1-10. The ToArray() Method in Action

```
List<Person> people = new List<Person> {
    new Person() { ID = 1,
                   IDRole = 1,
                   LastName = "Anderson",
                   FirstName = "Brad"},
    new Person() { ID = 2,
                   IDRole = 2,
                   LastName = "Gray",
                   FirstName = "Tom"}
        };
```

```
var query = people
           .Where (p => p.ID == 1)
           .Select( p => new { p.FirstName, p.LastName } )
           .ToArray();

ObjectDumper.Write(query);

people[0].FirstName = "Fabio";

ObjectDumper.Write(query);
```

In Listing 1-10 the code caches the result of a query using the **ToArray** method. As the output in Figure 1-4 shows, even if the code changes an element of the **List<T>** collection, the query returns the same result since it has been cached.

Figure 1-4. The output of the ToArray() example in Listing 1-10

Standard Query Operators

LINQ provides an API known as *standard query operators* (SQOs) to support the kinds of operations we're accustomed to in SQL. You've already used C#'s **select** and **where** keywords, which map to LINQ's **Select** and **Where** SQOs—which, like all SQOs, are actually methods of the **System.Linq.Enumerable** static class. Table 1-1 is a complete listing of SQOs.

Table 1-1. LINQ Standard Query Operators Grouped by Operation

OPERATION	OPERATOR	DESCRIPTION
Aggregate	Aggregate	Applies a function over a sequence
	Average	Calculates the average over a sequence
	Count/LongCount	Counts the element of a sequence
	Max	Returns the maximum value from a sequence of numeric values
	Min	Returns the minimum value from a sequence of numeric values
	Sum	Returns the sum of all numeric values from a sequence
Concatenation	Concat	Merges elements from two sequences
Conversion	AsEnumerable	Converts the sequence to a generic IEnumerable<T>
	AsQueryable	Converts the sequence to a generic IQueryable<T>
	Cast	Casts an element of the sequence into a specified type
	OfType	Filters elements of a sequence, returning only those of the specified type
	ToArray	Converts the sequence into an array
	ToDictionary	Creates a Dictionary<K,E> from a sequence
	ToList	Creates a List<T> from a sequence

Table 1-1. continued

OPERATION	OPERATOR	DESCRIPTION
	`ToLookup`	Creates a `Lookup<K,T>` from a sequence
	`ToSequence`	Returns its argument typed as `IEnumerable<T>`
Element	`DefaultIfEmpty`	Provides a default element for an empty sequence
	`ElementAt`	Returns the element at the specified index from a sequence
	`ElementAtOrDefault`	Similar to `ElementAt` but also returns a default element when the specified index is out of range
	`First`	Returns the first element in a sequence
	`FirstOrDefault`	Similar to `First` but also returns a default element when the first element in the sequence is not available
	`Last`	Returns the last element in a sequence
	`LastOrDefault`	Similar to `Last` but also returns a default element when the last element in the sequence is not available
	`Single`	Returns a sequences single element that satisfies a condition specified as an argument

OPERATION	OPERATOR	DESCRIPTION
	SingleOrDefault	Similar to Single but also returns a default value when the single element is not found in the sequence
Equality	SequenceEqual	Checks whether two sequences are equal
Generation	Empty	Returns an empty sequence for the specified data type
	Range	Generates a numeric sequence from a range of two numbers
	Repeat	Generates a sequence by repeating the provided element a specified number of times
Grouping	GroupBy	Groups the elements of a sequence
Join	GroupJoin	Performs a grouped join of two sequences based on matching keys
	Join	Performs an inner join of two sequences based on matching keys
Ordering	OrderBy	Orders the elements of the sequence according to one or more keys
	OrderByDescending	Similar to OrderBy but sorts the sequence inversely
	Reverse	Reverses the elements of the sequence
	ThenBy	Useful for specifying additional ordering keys after the first one specified by either the OrderBy or OrderByDescending operator

Table 1-1. continued

OPERATION	OPERATOR	DESCRIPTION
	ThenByDescending	Similar to ThenBy but sorts the sequence inversely
Partitioning	Skip	Skips a given number of elements from a sequence and then yields the remainder of the sequence
	SkipWhile	Similar to Skip but the numbers of elements to skip are defined by a Boolean condition
	Take	Takes a given number of elements from a sequence and skips the remainder of the sequence
	TakeWhile	Similar to Take but the numbers of elements to take are defined by a Boolean condition
Projection	Select	Defines the elements to pick in a sequence
	SelectMany	Performs a one-to-many-elements projection over a sequence
Quantifier	All	Checks all the elements of a sequence against the provided condition
	Any	Checks whether any element of the sequence satisfies the provided condition
	Contains	Checks for an element presence into a sequence

OPERATION	OPERATOR	DESCRIPTION
Restriction	Where	Filters a sequence based on the provided condition
Set	Distinct	Returns distinct elements from a sequence
	Except	Produces a sequence that is the difference between elements of two sequences
	Intersect	Produces a sequence resulting from the common elements of two sequences
	Union	Produces a sequence that is the union of two sequences

In the rest of this chapter we'll examine each operator carefully, and consider examples that illustrate the elements' functionality. The examples will be based on numeric sequences for operators that use numbers, and on classes such as **Person**, **Role**, and **Salary** for operators that use more-complex sequences. Listing 1-11 shows these classes.

Listing 1-11. The Person, Role, and Salary classes

```
class Person
{
    int _id;
    int _idRole;
    string _lastName;
    string _firstName;

    public int ID
    {
        get { return _id; }
        set { _id = value; }
    }
}
```

```csharp
    public int IDRole
    {
        get { return _idRole; }
        set { _idRole = value; }
    }

    public string LastName
    {
        get { return _lastName; }
        set { _lastName = value; }
    }

    public string FirstName
    {
        get { return _firstName; }
        set { _firstName = value; }
    }
}

class Role
{
    int _id;
    string _roleDescription;

    public int ID
    {
        get { return _id; }
        set { _id = value; }
    }

    public string RoleDescription
    {
        get { return _roleDescription; }
        set { _roleDescription = value; }
    }
}

class Salary
{
    int _idPerson;
    int _year;
    double _salary;
```

```
public int IDPerson
{
    get { return _idPerson; }
    set { _idPerson = value; }
}

public int Year
{
    get { return _year; }
    set { _year = value; }
}

public double SalaryYear
{
    get { return _salary; }
    set { _salary = value; }
}
}
```

The Person class provides four properties, one of which is the matching key with the second class, Role. The Role class provides two public properties to store the role identifier and its description. The Salary class provides the IDPerson foreign key to join to the Person class.

Let's now look at all the operators, starting with the most used ones.

Restriction Operator

There is one restriction operator: Where.

Where

One of the most used LINQ operators is Where. It restricts the sequence returned by a query based on a predicate provided as an argument.

```
public static IEnumerable<T> Where<T>(
    this IEnumerable<T> source, Func<T, bool> predicate);

public static IEnumerable<T> Where<T>(
    this IEnumerable<T> source, Func<T, int, bool> predicate);
```

The two forms differ in the second parameter, the predicate. It indicates the condition that has to be checked for each element of a sequence. The second form also accepts an int representing the zero-based index of the element of the source sequence.

Both operators extend the IEnumerable<T> type. Let's look at a couple of examples.

The code snippet in Listing 1-12 uses Where (through the C# where keyword) to retrieve every element in a sequence that has FirstName equal to Brad. Figure 1-5 shows the output.

Listing 1-12. The Where Operator in Action

```
List<Person> people = new List<Person> {
    new Person { ID = 1,
                 IDRole = 1,
                 LastName = "Anderson",
                 FirstName = "Brad"},
    new Person { ID = 2,
                 IDRole = 2,
                 LastName = "Gray",
                 FirstName = "Tom"},
    new Person { ID = 3,
                 IDRole = 2,
                 LastName = "Grant",
                 FirstName = "Mary"},
    new Person { ID = 4,
                 IDRole = 3,
                 LastName = "Cops",
                 FirstName = "Gary"}};

var query = from p in people
            where p.FirstName == "Brad"
            select p;
ObjectDumper.Write(query);
```

Figure 1-5. The output of Listing 1-12

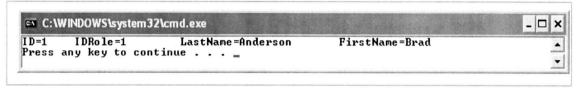

Listing 1-13 uses the second `Where` form.

Listing 1-13. Using Where with an Index

```csharp
List<Person> people = new List<Person> {
    new Person { ID = 1,
                 IDRole = 1,
                 LastName = "Anderson",
                 FirstName = "Brad"},
    new Person { ID = 2,
                 IDRole = 2,
                 LastName = "Gray",
                 FirstName = "Tom"},
    new Person { ID = 3,
                 IDRole = 2,
                 LastName = "Grant",
                 FirstName = "Mary"},
    new Person { ID = 4,
                 IDRole = 3,
                 LastName = "Cops",
                 FirstName = "Gary"}};

var query = people
            .Where((p, index) => p.IDRole == index);

ObjectDumper.Write(query);
```

In this case, the condition yields each sequence element whose index equals `IDRole`. The `people` data source shows that this is true only for the last element, as you can see in Figure 1-6.

Figure 1-6. The output for the Where example in Listing 1-13

```
C:\WINDOWS\system32\cmd.exe                                    _ □ ×
ID=3      IDRole=2        LastName=Grant   FirstName=Mary
ID=4      IDRole=3        LastName=Cops    FirstName=Gary
Press any key to continue . . . _
```

Projection Operators

There are two projection one operators: `Select` and `SelectMany`.

Select

Just like `SELECT` in SQL, the `Select` operator specifies which elements are to be retrieved.

```
public static IEnumerable<S> Select<T, S>(
    this IEnumerable<T> source, Func<T, S> selector);

public static IEnumerable<S> Select<T, S>(
    this IEnumerable<T> source, Func<T, int, S> selector);
```

Both operators extend the `IEnumerable<T>` type. They differ in the second parameter. The first form accepts a selector function, where we can define the element to pick; the second also accepts a zero-based index indicating the position of the element in the sequence. Let's look at a couple of examples. The code snippet in Listing 1-14 returns all the elements from the sequence, just like `SELECT *` in SQL. Figure 1-7 shows the output.

Listing 1-14. Using the First Form of Select

```
List<Person> people = new List<Person> {
    new Person { ID = 1,
                IDRole = 1,
                LastName = "Anderson",
                FirstName = "Brad"},
    new Person { ID = 2,
                IDRole = 2,
                LastName = "Gray",
```

```
                    FirstName = "Tom"},
    new Person { ID = 3,
                    IDRole = 2,
                    LastName = "Grant",
                    FirstName = "Mary"},
    new Person { ID = 4,
                    IDRole = 3,
                    LastName = "Cops",
                    FirstName = "Gary"}};
var query = from p in people
            select p;

ObjectDumper.Write(query);
```

Figure 1-7. The output of Listing 1-14

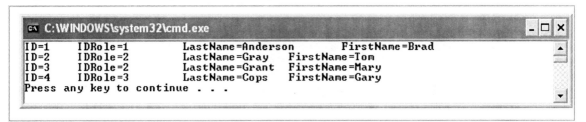

Listing 1-15 uses an index to specify the element position in the sequence.

Listing 1-15. Using an Index with Select

```
List<Person> people = new List<Person> {
    new Person { ID = 1,
                    IDRole = 1,
                    LastName = "Anderson",
                    FirstName = "Brad"},
    new Person { ID = 2,
                    IDRole = 2,
                    LastName = "Gray",
                    FirstName = "Tom"},
    new Person { ID = 3,
                    IDRole = 2,
                    LastName = "Grant",
                    FirstName = "Mary"},
    new Person { ID = 4,
                    IDRole = 3,
                    LastName = "Cops",
```

```
                    FirstName = "Gary"}};

var query = people
        .Select(
                (p,index) => new { Position=index,
                                  p.FirstName,
                                  p.LastName } );

ObjectDumper.Write(query);
```

This code snippet creates an anonymous type, formed by the full name of
the person anticipated by the element position in the sequence. See Figure
1-8 for the output.

Figure 1-8. The output of Listing 1-15

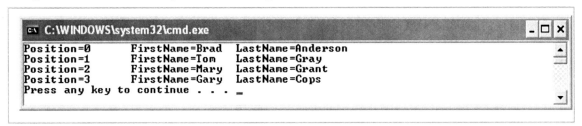

SelectMany

This operator is similar to Select because it allows us to define the
elements to pick from a sequence. The difference is in the return type.

```
public static IEnumerable<S> SelectMany<T, S>(
    this IEnumerable<T> source,
    Func<T, IEnumerable<S>> selector);

public static IEnumerable<S> SelectMany<T, S>(
    this IEnumerable<T> source,
    Func<T, int, IEnumerable<S>> selector);
```

With the IEnumerable<S> type returned by the selector parameter of
SelectMany, it's possible to concatenate many projection operations
together, either on different sequences or starting from the result of a
previous query.

The SelectMany operator extends the IEnumerable<T> type. The selector parameter has two formats: the first returns the IEnumerable<S> type and the second also requires a zero-based index that specifies the position of the element in the sequence. Listings 1-16 and 1-17 clarify the differences between Select and SelectMany.

Listing 1-16. The SelectMany Method in Action

```
List<Person> people = new List<Person> {
    new Person { ID = 1,
                 IDRole = 1,
                 LastName = "Anderson",
                 FirstName = "Brad"},
    new Person { ID = 2,
                 IDRole = 2,
                 LastName = "Gray",
                 FirstName = "Tom"},
    new Person { ID = 3,
                 IDRole = 2,
                 LastName = "Grant",
                 FirstName = "Mary"},
    new Person { ID = 4,
                 IDRole = 3,
                 LastName = "Cops",
                 FirstName = "Gary"}};


List<Role> roles = new List<Role> {
    new Role { ID = 1, RoleDescription = "Manager" },
    new Role { ID = 2, RoleDescription = "Developer" }};

var query = from p in people
            where p.ID == 1
            from r in roles
            where r.ID == p.IDRole
            select new { p.FirstName,
                         p.LastName,
                         r.RoleDescription };

ObjectDumper.Write(query);
```

This code snippet obtains a result similar to a database join, where the result of the first query is used in the other sequence to obtain the element corresponding to the match condition. It's interesting to analyze how the compiler transforms the query expression pattern used in Listing 1-16 to generate the operator method call (see Listing 1-17). Figure 1-9 shows the output.

Listing 1-17. Listing 1-16 After Transformation

```
var query = people
          .Where(p => p.ID == 1)
          .SelectMany(p => roles
          .Where(r => r.ID == p.ID)
          .Select(r => new { p.FirstName,
                             p.LastName,
                             r.RoleDescription}));
```

Figure 1-9. The output of Listings 1-16 and 1-17

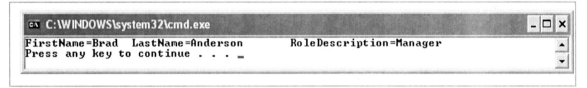

SelectMany allows us to manage another sequence since it returns an IEnumerable<S>, where S is the sequence. If we use the Select operator instead of SelectMany, we will get an IEnumerable<List<T>>. This object is not composed of the sequence but of List<T> elements.

Join Operators

There are two join operators: Join and GroupJoin.

Join

Like INNER JOIN in SQL, the Join operator combines two sequences based on matching keys supplied as arguments. The Join operator is not overloaded.

```
public static IEnumerable<V> Join<T, U, K, V>(
    this IEnumerable<T> outer,
    IEnumerable<U> inner,
    Func<T, K> outerKeySelector,
    Func<U, K> innerKeySelector,
    Func<T, U, V> resultSelector);
```

The Join operator extends the IEnumerable<T> type. The first parameter is one of the two sequences to join. It will be evaluated against the function specified as the outerKeySelector parameter. The second parameter contains the inner sequence used during the evaluation of the inner elements against the function specified as the innerKeySelector parameter. For each matching inner element the resultSelector function, specified as the last parameter, is evaluated for the outer and inner element pair, and the resulting object is returned. Listing 1-18 provides an example. Figure 1-10 shows the output.

Listing 1-18. The Join Operator in Action

```
List<Person> people = new List<Person> {
    new Person { ID = 1,
                 IDRole = 1,
                 LastName = "Anderson",
                 FirstName = "Brad"},
    new Person { ID = 2,
                 IDRole = 2,
                 LastName = "Gray",
                 FirstName = "Tom"},
    new Person { ID = 3,
                 IDRole = 2,
                 LastName = "Grant",
                 FirstName = "Mary"},
    new Person { ID = 4,
                 IDRole = 3,
                 LastName = "Cops",
                 FirstName = "Gary"}};
```

```
List<Role> roles = new List<Role> {
  new Role { ID = 1, RoleDescription = "Manager" },
  new Role { ID = 2, RoleDescription = "Developer" }};

var query = from p in people
            join r in roles on p.IDRole equals r.ID
            select new { p.FirstName,
                         p.LastName,
                         r.RoleDescription };

ObjectDumper.Write(query);
```

Figure 1-10. The output of Listing 1-18

```
C:\WINDOWS\system32\cmd.exe                                    _ □ ×
FirstName=Brad   LastName=Anderson        RoleDescription=Manager
FirstName=Tom    LastName=Gray   RoleDescription=Developer
FirstName=Mary   LastName=Grant  RoleDescription=Developer
Press any key to continue . . .
```

GroupJoin

This operator is similar to Join but it returns the result in an IEnumerable<S>
where S is a new sequence.

```
public static IEnumerable<V> GroupJoin<T, U, K, V>(
    this IEnumerable<T> outer,
    IEnumerable<U> inner,
    Func<T, K> outerKeySelector,
    Func<U, K> innerKeySelector,
    Func<T, IEnumerable<U>, V> resultSelector);
```

This operator is really useful when we have to implement particular joins,
such as SQL's LEFT OUTER join. Listing 1-19 provides and example:

Listing 1-19. GroupJoin in Action

```
List<Person> people = new List<Person> {
    new Person { ID = 1,
                 IDRole = 1,
                 LastName = "Anderson",
```

```
                    FirstName = "Brad"},
    new Person { ID = 2,
                 IDRole = 2,
                 LastName = "Gray",
                 FirstName = "Tom"},
    new Person { ID = 3,
                 IDRole = 2,
                 LastName = "Grant",
                 FirstName = "Mary"},
    new Person { ID = 4,
                 IDRole = 3,
                 LastName = "Cops",
                 FirstName = "Gary"}};

List<Role> roles = new List<Role> {
    new Role { ID = 1, RoleDescription = "Manager" },
    new Role { ID = 2, RoleDescription = "Developer" }};

var query = from p in people
            join r in roles on p.IDRole equals r.ID into pr
            from r in pr.DefaultIfEmpty()
            select new { p.FirstName,
                         p.LastName,
                         RoleDescription = r == null ?
                            "No Role" : r.RoleDescription
                       };

ObjectDumper.Write(query);
```

In the code snippet in Listing 1-19 the `join … into` query expression is used to group the join into a new sequence called `pr`. Since the new element we introduced in the `people` sequence has a role identifier that doesn't correspond to any of `Role` elements in the `roles` sequence, an empty element is returned. Using the `DefaultIfEmpty` method, we can replace each empty element with the given ones. In this case no parameter has been provided, so the empty element will be replaced with a `null` value. By checking this value in the `select` command we can provide a custom description (`"No Role"` in our case) when the code encounters `null` elements. See the output in Figure 1-11.

Figure 1-11. The output of Listing 1-19

```
C:\WINDOWS\system32\cmd.exe                                      _ □ ×
FirstName=Brad   LastName=Anderson        RoleDescription=Manager
FirstName=Tom    LastName=Gray     RoleDescription=Developer
FirstName=Mary   LastName=Grant    RoleDescription=Developer
FirstName=Gary   LastName=Cops     RoleDescription=No Role
Press any key to continue . . . _
```

Grouping Operator

There is one grouping operator: GroupBy.

GroupBy

Just like the GROUP BY clause of SQL, the GroupBy operator groups elements of a sequence based on a given selector function.

```
public static IEnumerable<IGrouping<K, T>> GroupBy<T, K>(
    this IEnumerable<T> source,
    Func<T, K> keySelector);

public static IEnumerable<IGrouping<K, T>> GroupBy<T, K>(
    this IEnumerable<T> source,
    Func<T, K> keySelector,
    IEqualityComparer<K> comparer);

public static IEnumerable<IGrouping<K, E>> GroupBy<T, K, E>(
    this IEnumerable<T> source,
    Func<T, K> keySelector,
    Func<T, E> elementSelector);

public static IEnumerable<IGrouping<K, E>> GroupBy<T, K, E>(
    this IEnumerable<T> source,
    Func<T, K> keySelector,
    Func<T, E> elementSelector,
    IEqualityComparer<K> comparer);
```

Each GroupBy operator returns an IEnumerable<IGrouping<K, E>>. Let's look at how IGrouping<K, T> is declared:

```
public interface IGrouping<K, T> : IEnumerable<T>
{
    K Key { get; }
}
```

This interface implements `IEnumerable<T>` and adds a read-only property called `Key`. When the code process launches the query (that is when we are going to iterate through elements using a `foreach` statement) the `source` parameter is enumerated and evaluated against the `keySelector` and `elementSelector` functions (if specified). When every element has been evaluated and each element that satisfies the selector functions has been collected, new instances of the `IGrouping<K, E>` type are yielded. Finally, the `IEqualityComparer` interface, when specified, allows us to define a new way to compare elements of a sequence. Let's look at the example in Listing 1-20.

Listing 1-20. An Example of GroupBy Using .NET Reflection

```
var query = from m in typeof(int).GetMethods()
            select m.Name;

ObjectDumper.Write(query);

Console.WriteLine("-=-=-=-=-=-=-=-=");
Console.WriteLine("After the GroupBy");
Console.WriteLine("-=-=-=-=-=-=-=-=");

var q = from m in typeof(int).GetMethods()
        group m by m.Name into gb
        select new {Name = gb.Key};

ObjectDumper.Write(q);
```

The first query expression calls the `GetMethods` method provided by .NET Reflection to retrieve the list of available methods for the `int` type. Since `GetMethods()` returns a `MethodInfo[]` array LINQ query expressions could use it easily too. The first part of the output shows the methods for the `int` type without the grouping (see Figure 1-12). The second part of the code snippet in Listing 1-20 uses the group by clause to group the elements by method name. The result of the group by clause is inserted into the new IGrouping<K, E> type that provides the Key property representing the by argument of the group by operator. Since the method's name has been promoted to a grouping key, the Key property will be equal to the method's name.

Figure 1-12. The output of Listing 1-20

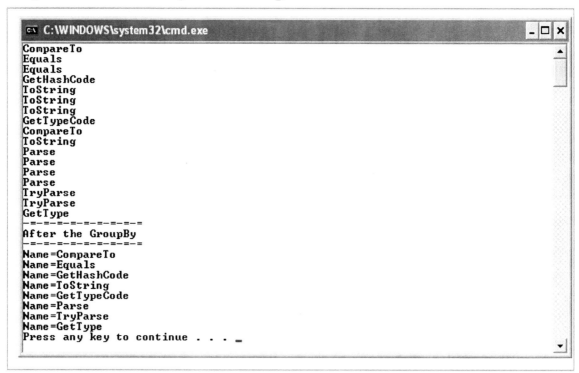

In Listing 1-21 I added the Count operator to compute the number of method overloads.

Listing 1-21. Another Example of group by Clause

```
var q = from m in typeof(int).GetMethods()
        group m by m.Name into gb
```

```
        select new {Name = gb.Key, Overloads = gb.Count()};

ObjectDumper.Write(q);
```

The **gb** variable represents the result of the **group by** operation; it's possible
to operate against this variable to filter its element, specify a **where** clause,
and so on. In this case the code snippet shows the result of counting the
number of elements for each key in the group. In this case it represents the
method's overloads. See Figure 1-13 for the output.

Figure 1-13. The output of Listing 1-21

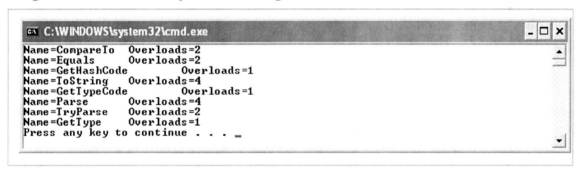

The last example for the grouping operator uses the **comparer** parameter,
which allows us to customize the behavior of the **GroupBy** method during its
work. See Listing 1-22.

*Listing 1-22. The GroupBy Operator with a Custom Comparison
Method*

```
    public class MyComparer : IEqualityComparer<string>
    {
        public bool Equals(string x, string y) {
            return (x.Substring(0,2)) == (y.Substring(0,2));
        }

        public int GetHashCode(string obj) {
            return (obj.Substring(0,2)).GetHashCode();
        }
    }
```

```
string[] dictionary = new string[] {"F:Apple", "F:Banana",
                                    "T:House", "T:Phone",
                                    "F:Cherry", "T:Computer"};
var query = dictionary.GroupBy(d => d, new MyComparer());

ObjectDumper.Write(query, 1);
```

The **dictionary** array contains two kinds of objects. The F: prefix stands for *fruit* and the T: prefix stands for *thing*. We have defined a way to group fruit with fruit and thing with thing. To create a custom comparer we have to define a new class that implements the **IEqualityComparer<T>** interface. The contract subordinated by this interface forces us to implement two methods: **Equals** and **GetHashCode**. For **Equals** we have to insert the custom logic for our comparer. **GetHashCode** has to return the hash code for the same string checked in the **Equals** method. In Listing 1-22 we have a simple way to check the category of the strings. By analyzing their first two characters we know that F: stands for *fruit* and T: stands for *thing*. We simply have to check that both strings provided to the **Equals** method contain the same substring. Figure 1-14 shows the output for Listing 1-22.

Figure 1-14. We have grouped fruits and things.

```
C:\WINDOWS\system32\cmd.exe
. . .
  F:Apple
  F:Banana
  F:Cherry
. . .
  T:House
  T:Phone
  T:Computer
Press any key to continue . . .
```

Ordering Operators

There are five ordering operators: OrderBy, OrderByDescending, ThenBy, ThenByDescending, and Reverse.

OrderBy and OrderByDescending

Like ORDER BY and ORDER BY DESC in SQL, the OrderBy and OrderByDescending operators order elements of a sequence according to a given key. The OrderByDescending operator inverts the ordering.

```
public static OrderedSequence<T> OrderBy<T, K>(
    this IEnumerable<T> source,
    Func<T, K> keySelector);

public static OrderedSequence<T> OrderBy<T, K>(
    this IEnumerable<T> source,
    Func<T, K> keySelector,
    IComparer<K> comparer);

public static OrderedSequence<T> OrderByDescending<T, K>(
    this IEnumerable<T> source,
    Func<T, K> keySelector);

public static OrderedSequence<T> OrderByDescending<T, K>(
    this IEnumerable<T> source,
    Func<T, K> keySelector,
    IComparer<K> comparer);
```

The keySelector parameter is used to extract the elements from the sequence. When specified the comparer parameter compares the elements. When the code processes the query, the method collects all the elements and evaluates each of them against the keySelector. Finally, an OrderedSequence<T> type is produced. This is similar to IEnumerable<T> except that it doesn't provide public methods. Listing 1-23 provides an example.

```
var q = from m in typeof(int).GetMethods()
        orderby m.Name
        group m by m.Name into gb
        select new {Name = gb.Key};

ObjectDumper.Write(q);
```

The code snippet in Listing 1-23 retrieves the int type's methods ordered by their names. See Figure 1-15 for the output.

Figure 1-15. The output for Listing 1-23

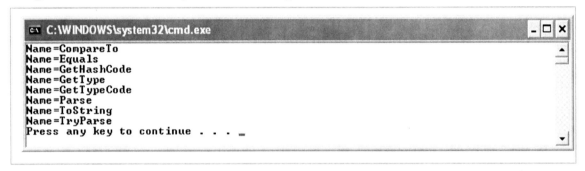

To obtain descending order, you simply add the descending keyword.

```
orderby m.Name descending
```

ThenBy and ThenByDescending

As you saw in the previous section, orderby allows us to specify only one ordering key. We have to use either ThenBy or ThenByDescending to concatenate ordering-key values.

```
public static OrderedSequence<T> ThenBy<T, K>(
    this OrderedSequence<T> source,
    Func<T, K> keySelector);

public static OrderedSequence<T> ThenBy<T, K>(
    this OrderedSequence<T> source,
    Func<T, K> keySelector,
```

```
    IComparer<K> comparer);

public static OrderedSequence<T> ThenByDescending<T, K>(
    this OrderedSequence<T> source,
    Func<T, K> keySelector);

public static OrderedSequence<T> ThenByDescending<T, K>(
    this OrderedSequence<T> source,
    Func<T, K> keySelector,
    IComparer<K> comparer);
```

Just like in the `OrderBy` operators, the first argument is the source sequence whose elements are evaluated against the `keySelector` parameter. Listing 1-24 shows a more complete `OrderBy`/`ThenBy` example.

Listing 1-24. The OrderBy and ThenBy Operators

```
List<Person> people = new List<Person> {
    new Person { ID = 1,
                 IDRole = 1,
                 LastName = "Anderson",
                 FirstName = "Brad"},
    new Person { ID = 2,
                 IDRole = 2,
                 LastName = "Gray",
                 FirstName = "Tom"},
    new Person { ID = 3,
                 IDRole = 2,
                 LastName = "Grant",
                 FirstName = "Mary"},
    new Person { ID = 4,
                 IDRole = 3,
                 LastName = "Cops",
                 FirstName = "Gary"}};


var query = from p in people
            orderby p.FirstName, p.LastName
            select p;

ObjectDumper.Write(query);
```

When the compiler encounters the query pattern in Listing 1-24 it transforms the first argument of the **orderby** operator to a call to the OrderBy() method, and transforms every other parameter after the comma to a related ThenBy() method call.

```
var query = people.OrderBy(p => p.FirstName).
                ThenBy(p => p.LastName);
```

Figure 1-16 shows the output of this code snippet.

Figure 1-16. The output of the ordered sequence shown in Listing 1-24

```
C:\WINDOWS\system32\cmd.exe

ID=1       IDRole=1          LastName=Anderson        FirstName=Brad
ID=4       IDRole=3          LastName=Cops      FirstName=Gary
ID=3       IDRole=2          LastName=Grant     FirstName=Mary
ID=2       IDRole=2          LastName=Gray      FirstName=Tom
Press any key to continue . . .
```

The last example on the ordering operators uses the comparer function (see Listing 1-25).

Listing 1-25. Using the comparer Function to Customize the Ordering Behavior

```csharp
public class MyOrderingComparer : IComparer<string>
{
    public int Compare(string x, string y)
    {
        x = x.Replace("_",string.Empty);
        y = y.Replace("_",string.Empty);

        return string.Compare(x, y);
    }
}

string[] dictionary = new string[] {"Apple",
                                    "Banana",
                                    "Cherry"};
var query = dictionary.OrderBy(w => w,
```

```
                    new MyOrderingComparer());

ObjectDumper.Write(query);
```

To use the comparer parameter function we have to create a new class that
implements the `IComparer<T>` interface. Its contract forces us to define the
`Compare()` method, then add the comparing logic. In the code snippet in
Listing 1-25 we want to treat the underscored string as a normal string
when the ordering is implemented. So just before the `Compare()` method is
called in the comparer function, we will remove each underscore from the
source strings. See the output in Figure 1-17.

*Figure 1-17. A custom comparer function allows us to change the
ordering of the strings.*

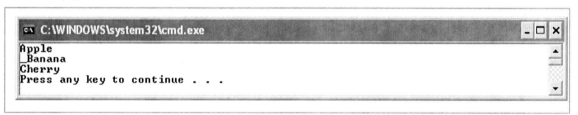

Note   The May 2006 CTP release doesn't provide support for ordering
operators with Visual Studio 2005 IntelliSense.

Reverse

This method simply returns a new sequence with elements in reverse
ordering of the source sequence.

```
public static IEnumerable<T> Reverse<T>(
    this IEnumerable<T> source);
```

When the code processes the query expression, the method enumerates the
elements of the source sequence, collecting them in an `IEnumerable<T>` type.

Before the method returns the result it inverts the ordering of the elements in the sequence.

Aggregate Operators

There are seven aggregate operators: Count, LongCount, Sum, Min, Max, Average and Aggregate.

Count and LongCount

Those methods return the number of elements within a sequence. The difference between them is in the return type. The Count() method returns an integer and the LongCount() method returns a long type. Let's see the methods' prototypes:

```
public static int Count<T>(
    this IEnumerable<T> source);

public static int Count<T>(
    this IEnumerable<T> source,
    Func<T, bool> predicate);

public static long LongCount<T>(
    this IEnumerable<T> source);

public static long LongCount<T>(
    this IEnumerable<T> source,
    Func<T, bool> predicate);
```

Both methods have two different prototypes. The former, without the predicate parameter, checks the type of the source parameter. If it implements the ICollection<T> type then its Count method is used. If it doesn't, the source sequence is enumerated, incrementing a number that represents the final count value. The latter uses the predicate function parameter returning the count of elements against which the specified condition is true.

We have already used the Count operator in the "Grouping Operators" section; see Listing 1-21 for an example of the Count operator.

Sum

The Sum method computes the sum of numeric values within a sequence.

```
public static Numeric Sum(
    this IEnumerable<Numeric> source);

public static Numeric Sum<T>(
    this IEnumerable<T> source,
    Func<T, Numeric> selector);
```

The Numeric type returned from the Sum() method must be one of the following: int, int?, long, long?, double, double?, decimal, or decimal?.

Note   The ? suffix to the primitive type name specifies that a variable of that type can contain null values. This feature was added to .NET 2.0 to provide greater compatibility with NULLABLE columns in database tables.

The first prototype without the **selector** parameter computes the sum of the elements in the sequence. When the **selector** parameter is used it picks the specified element of the sequence on which computing the sum will start. The Sum operator does not include null values in the result, which means a zero will be returned for an empty sequence (see Listing 1-26).

Listing 1-26. A Code Snippet for the Sum Operator

```
int[] numbers = { 1, 2, 3, 4, 5, 6, 7, 8, 9 };
var query = numbers.Sum();
ObjectDumper.Write(query);
```

The output for the code snippet in Listing 1-26 will be the sum of all the elements in the sequence: 45.

Another great use for the Sum operator is to have it work with the GroupBy operator to obtain total salary amounts, like the one shown in Listing 1-27.

Listing 1-27. Using Sum and GroupBy Operators to Obtain Salary Results

```
List<Person> people = new List<Person> {
    new Person { ID = 1,
                IDRole = 1,
                LastName = "Anderson",
                FirstName = "Brad"},
    new Person { ID = 2,
                IDRole = 2,
                LastName = "Gray",
                FirstName = "Tom"},
    new Person { ID = 3,
                IDRole = 2,
                LastName = "Grant",
                FirstName = "Mary"},
    new Person { ID = 4,
                IDRole = 3,
                LastName = "Cops",
                FirstName = "Gary"}};

List<Salary> salaries = new List<Salary> {
    new Salary { IDPerson = 1,
                Year = 2004,
                SalaryYear = 10000.00 },
    new Salary { IDPerson = 1,
                Year = 2005,
                SalaryYear = 15000.00 }};

var query = from p in people
            join s in salaries on p.ID equals s.IDPerson
            select new { p.FirstName,
                        p.LastName,
                        s.SalaryYear };

var querySum = from q in query
            group q by q.LastName into gp
            select new { LastName = gp.Key,
                        TotalSalary =
```

```
                    gp.Sum(q => q.SalaryYear) };

ObjectDumper.Write(querySum,1);
```

The **salaries** collection contains the total salary per year. The record is related to the **people** collection through the **IDPerson** attribute.

The first query joins the two sequences, returning a new anonymous type composed of a person's name and salary. The result is processed again by another query expression, which groups by the **LastName** attribute and returns a new anonymous type with the total salary for that person. See Figure 1-18 for the output.

Figure 1-18. The output for Listing 1-27

Min and Max

The **Min()** and **Max()** methods return the minimum and the maximum element within a sequence, respectively.

```
public static Numeric Min(
    this IEnumerable<Numeric> source);

public static T Min<T>(
    this IEnumerable<T> source);
public static Numeric Min<T>(
    this IEnumerable<T> source,
    Func<T, Numeric> selector);

public static S Min<T, S>(
    this IEnumerable<T> source,
    Func<T, S> selector);
public static Numeric Max(
    this IEnumerable<Numeric> source);
```

```
public static T Max<T>(
    this IEnumerable<T> source);

public static Numeric Max<T>(
    this IEnumerable<T> source,
    Func<T, Numeric> selector);

public static S Max<T, S>(
    this IEnumerable<T> source,
    Func<T, S> selector);
```

When the code processes the query expression, the Min and Max operators enumerate the source sequence and call the selector for each element, finding the minimum and maximum. When no selector function is specified, the minimum and the maximum are calculated by elements themselves.

Listing 1-28 shows retrieval of the minimum and the maximum salary for the Brad Anders person element.

Listing 1-28. Using the Min and Max Operators to Retrieve the Minimum and Maximum Salary

```
List<Person> people = new List<Person> {
    new Person { ID = 1,
                 IDRole = 1,
                 LastName = "Anderson",
                 FirstName = "Brad"},
    new Person { ID = 2,
                 IDRole = 2,
                 LastName = "Gray",
                 FirstName = "Tom"},
    new Person { ID = 3,
                 IDRole = 2,
                 LastName = "Grant",
                 FirstName = "Mary"},
    new Person { ID = 4,
                 IDRole = 3,
                 LastName = "Cops",
                 FirstName = "Gary"}};
```

```
List<Salary> salaries = new List<Salary> {
    new Salary { IDPerson = 1, Year = 2004, SalaryYear = 10000.00 },
    new Salary { IDPerson = 1, Year = 2005, SalaryYear = 15000.00 }};

var query = from p in people
            join s in salaries on p.ID equals s.IDPerson
            where p.ID == 1
            select s.SalaryYear;

Console.WriteLine("Minimum Salary:");
ObjectDumper.Write(query.Min());

Console.WriteLine("Maximum Salary:");
ObjectDumper.Write(query.Max());
```

From the query expression we retrieve the salaries for the person that has
the identifier equal to 1 and then we apply the Min and Max operators to the
result. See Figure 1-19 for the output.

*Figure 1-19. The Min and Max operators prompting the minimum
and maximum salary*

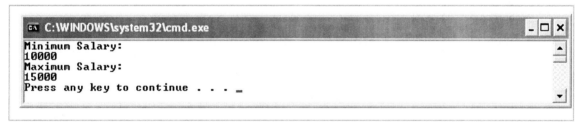

Average

This operator computes the average of the elements within a sequence.

```
public static Result Average(
    this IEnumerable<Numeric> source);

public static Result Average<T>(
    this IEnumerable<T> source,
    Func<T, Numeric> selector);
```

The `Result` type returned from the preceding prototypes will be either a `double` or `double?` type when the `Numeric` type is `int` and `long` or `int?` and `long?`, respectively. When the `Numeric` type assumes other types, those will be returned as is.

When the average is computed, if the sum of the elements is too large to be contained in the `Numeric` type an overflow exception will be thrown. Listing 1-29 shows the operator in action.

Listing 1-29. Using the Average Operator to Compute the Average of the Salary

```
List<Person> people = new List<Person> {
    new Person { ID = 1,
                 IDRole = 1,
                 LastName = "Anderson",
                 FirstName = "Brad"},
    new Person { ID = 2,
                 IDRole = 2,
                 LastName = "Gray",
                 FirstName = "Tom"},
    new Person { ID = 3,
                 IDRole = 2,
                 LastName = "Grant",
                 FirstName = "Mary"},
    new Person { ID = 4,
                 IDRole = 3,
                 LastName = "Cops",
                 FirstName = "Gary"}};

List<Salary> salaries = new List<Salary> {
    new Salary { IDPerson = 1, Year = 2004, SalaryYear = 10000.00 },
    new Salary { IDPerson = 1, Year = 2005, SalaryYear = 15000.00 }};

var query = from p in people
            join s in salaries on p.ID equals s.IDPerson
            where p.ID == 1
            select s.SalaryYear;

Console.WriteLine("Average Salary:");
ObjectDumper.Write(query.Average());
```

From the query expression we retrieve the salaries for the person that has the identifier equal to 1 and then we apply the Average method to the result. See Figure 1-20 for the output.

See Figure 1-20 for the output.

Figure 1-20. The output for Listing 1-29

Aggregate

This operator allows us to define a function used during the aggregation of the elements of a sequence.

```
public static T Aggregate<T>(
    this IEnumerable<T> source,
    Func<T, T, T> func);

public static U Aggregate<T, U>(
    this IEnumerable<T> source,
    U seed,
    Func<U, T, U> func);
```

The difference between those two prototypes stands in the seed parameter. When it is not specified the method uses the specified function to aggregate the elements of the sequence, assuming the first element as seed. When seed is specified the operator uses the seed value as a starting point for applying the aggregate function. Let's look at an example in Listing 1-30:

Listing 1-30. The Aggregate Method in Action

```
int[] numbers = { 1, 2, 3, 4, 5, 6, 7, 8, 9 };
var query = numbers.Aggregate((a,b) => a * b);
ObjectDumper.Write(query);
```

This code snippet uses the method without the **seed** parameter, so it takes the first element, 1, as seed, multiplying it for each other element in the sequence. The final result will be 362880.

In Listing 1-31 we will use the **seed** parameter.

Listing 1-31. The Aggregate Method Used with the seed Parameter

```
int[] numbers = { 9, 3, 5, 4, 2, 6, 7, 1, 8 };
var query = numbers.Aggregate(5, (a,b) => ( (a < b) ? (a * b) : a));
ObjectDumper.Write(query);
```

The method starts evaluating 5 with the first element in the sequence, 9. Since we have defined a rule where the element in the sequence is multiplied by the **seed** only if it is greater than the aggregated value, the method multiplies those two values, producing 45. This new value will be greater than any of the other elements in the sequence, so the final result will be 45.

Partitioning Operators

There are four partitioning operators: `Take`, `Skip`, `TakeWhile`, and `SkipWhile`.

Take

The `Take` method returns a given number of elements within a sequence and ignores the rest.

```
public static IEnumerable<T> Take<T>(
    this IEnumerable<T> source,
    int count);
```

When the code processes the query expression, the source sequence is enumerated. This yields elements until the `count` parameter value is reached.

The `Take` and `Skip` methods are really useful when you need to implement a pagination-record mechanism. Listing 1-32 shows an easy approach to the pagination of elements within a sequence.

Listing 1-32. Take and Skip Methods to Reproduce a Pagination Mechanism

```
int[] numbers = {1, 2, 3, 4, 5, 6, 7, 8, 9};
var query = numbers.Take(5);
ObjectDumper.Write(query);
Console.Write("Press Enter key to see the other elements...");
Console.ReadLine();
var query2 = numbers.Skip(5);
ObjectDumper.Write(query2);
```

The first query yields just the first five elements of the sequence. After the Enter key is pressed another query is called, in which the Skip method ignores the first five elements, prompting the rest (see Figure 1-21).

Figure 1-21. The output for Listing 1-32

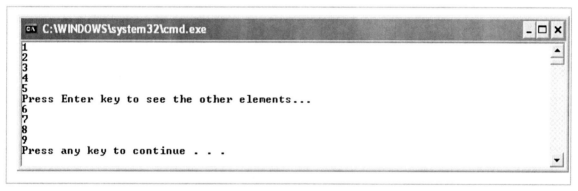

Skip

This method skips a given number of elements within a sequence, yielding the rest.

```
public static IEnumerable<T> Skip<T>(
    this IEnumerable<T> source,
    int count);
```

When the code processes the query expression the source sequence is enumerated, skipping elements until the count parameter value is reached.

See Listing 1-32 and Figure 1-21 for a Skip-method example.

TakeWhile

This method returns the elements from a sequence while the predicate function specified is true.

```
public static IEnumerable<T> TakeWhile<T>(
    this IEnumerable<T> source,
    Func<T, bool> predicate);

public static IEnumerable<T> TakeWhile<T>(
    this IEnumerable<T> source,
    Func<T, int, bool> predicate);
```

When the code processes the query expression the source sequence is enumerated, testing each element against the predicate function. Each element that satisfies the condition is yielded. The second prototype provides a zero-based index related to the elements of the sequence.

Listing 1-33 provides an example of the TakeWhile and SkipWhile methods.

Listing 1-33. The TakeWhile and SkipWhile Methods in Action

```
int[] numbers = { 9, 3, 5, 4, 2, 6, 7, 1, 8 };
var query = numbers.TakeWhile((n, index) => n >= index);
ObjectDumper.Write(query);
Console.Write("Press Enter key to see the other elements...");
Console.ReadLine();
var query2 = numbers.SkipWhile((n, index) => n >= index);
ObjectDumper.Write(query2);
```

This code snippet uses the TakeWhile second prototype, where the index of the elements of the sequence acts as a condition of the predicate function. Until the element's index is less than or equal to its own value, it is yielded. The rest of the elements will be skipped. After the Enter key is pressed the SkipWhile method is used with the same predicate condition to yield the other elements. See Figure 1-22 for the resulting output.

Figure 1-22. The output for Listing 1-33

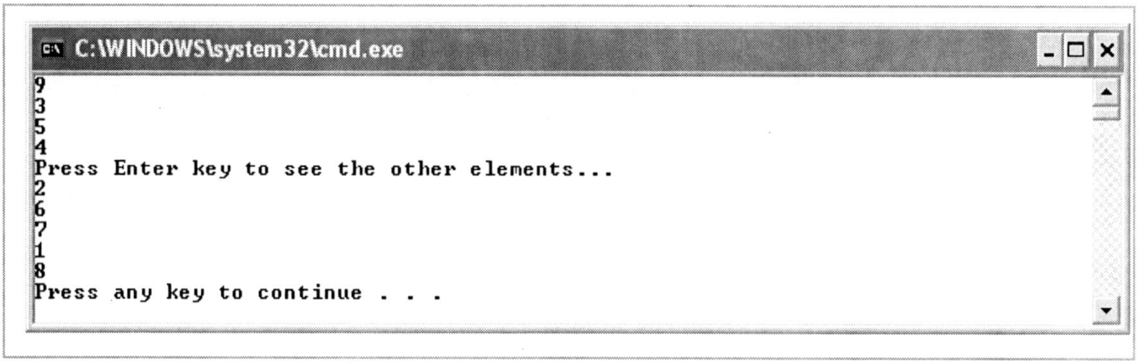

```
C:\WINDOWS\system32\cmd.exe                                    _ □ ×
9
3
5
4
Press Enter key to see the other elements...
2
6
7
1
8
Press any key to continue . . .
```

SkipWhile

The SkipWhile operator skips elements from a sequence while the predicate function returns true, then it yields the rest.

```
public static IEnumerable<T> SkipWhile<T>(
    this IEnumerable<T> source,
    Func<T, bool> predicate);

public static IEnumerable<T> SkipWhile<T>(
    this IEnumerable<T> source,
    Func<T, int, bool> predicate);
```

Each source element is tested against the predicate function parameter. The element will be skipped if the predicate function returns true. The second prototype provides a zero-based index related to the elements of the sequence.

For an example of the SkipWhile method see Listing 1-33.

Concatenation Operator

There is one concatenation operator: Concat.

Concat

This operator concatenates two sequences.

```
public static IEnumerable<T> Concat<T>(
    this IEnumerable<T> first,
    IEnumerable<T> second);
```

The resulting IEnumerable<T> type is the concatenation of the first and second sequences specified as a parameter.

In Listing 1-34 two numeric sequences are concatenated.

Listing 1-34. The Concat Method Used to Concatenate Two Numeric Sequences

```
int[] numbers = {1, 2, 3, 4, 5, 6, 7, 8, 9};
int[] moreNumbers = {10, 11, 12, 13};
var query = numbers.Concat(moreNumbers);
ObjectDumper.Write(query);
```

Starting from the numbers sequence the Concat method appends the moreNumbers sequence (see Figure 1-23).

Figure 1-23. The output of Listing 1-34

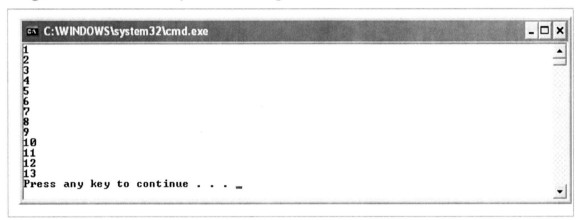

Element Operators

There are nine element operators: First, FirstOrDefault, Last, LastOrDefault, Single, SingleOrDefault, ElementAt, ElementAtOrDefault, and DefaultIfEmpty.

First, Last, FirstOrDefault, and LastOrDefault

These operators return the first/last element from a sequence.

```
public static T First<T>(
    this IEnumerable<T> source);

public static T First<T>(
    this IEnumerable<T> source,
    Func<T, bool> predicate);

public static T FirstOrDefault<T>(
    this IEnumerable<T> source);

public static T FirstOrDefault<T>(
    this IEnumerable<T> source,
    Func<T, bool> predicate);

public static T Last<T>(
    this IEnumerable<T> source);

public static T Last<T>(
    this IEnumerable<T> source,
    Func<T, bool> predicate);

public static T LastOrDefault<T>(
    this IEnumerable<T> source);

public static T LastOrDefault<T>(
    this IEnumerable<T> source,
    Func<T, bool> predicate);
```

When the **predicate** function parameter is specified, the method returns the first/last element against which the **predicate** function is satisfied, and therefore returns **true**. Otherwise the method returns simply the first/last element in the sequence. Listing 1-35 provides some examples.

Listing 1-35. Examples of the First and Last Methods

```
int[] numbers = {1, 2, 3, 4, 5, 6, 7, 8, 9};
var query = numbers.First();
Console.WriteLine("The first element in the sequence");
ObjectDumper.Write(query);
query = numbers.Last();
Console.WriteLine("The last element in the sequence");
ObjectDumper.Write(query);
Console.WriteLine("The first even element in the sequence");
query = numbers.First(n => n % 2 == 0);
ObjectDumper.Write(query);
Console.WriteLine("The last even element in the sequence");
query = numbers.Last(n => n % 2 == 0);
ObjectDumper.Write(query);
```

In Listing 1-35 the First and Last methods are used to retrieve the first and last element of the numeric sequence, respectively. Moreover, when the predicate function is specified the First and Last methods return the first and last even element, respectively (see Figure 1-24).

Figure 1-24. Sample output of the First and Last methods

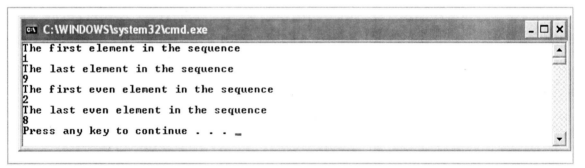

Using the FirstOrDefault/LastOrDefault methods we would have obtained the same results. However, when we use those methods and a predicate does not find an element satisfying the specified condition, a default value is returned (thereby avoiding retrieval of an exception). See the example in Listing 1-36.

Listing 1-36. A FirstOrDefault/LastOrDefault Example

```
int[] numbers = {1, 3, 5, 7, 9};
var query = numbers.FirstOrDefault(n => n % 2 == 0);
Console.WriteLine("The first even element in the sequence");
ObjectDumper.Write(query);
Console.WriteLine("The last odd element in the sequence");
query = numbers.LastOrDefault(n => n % 2 == 1);
ObjectDumper.Write(query);
```

Since no even numbers are in the sequence, `FirstOrDefault` returns the zero default value. On the other hand, the `LastOrDefault` operator looks for the last odd number in the sequence and finds the number 9. Figure 1-25 shows the output.

Figure 1-25. The output for Listing 1-36

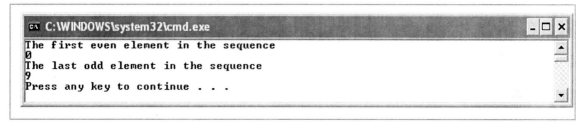

Single and SingleOrDefault

These methods return a single element picked from a sequence.

```
public static T Single<T>(
    this IEnumerable<T> source);

public static T Single<T>(
    this IEnumerable<T> source,
    Func<T, bool> predicate);

public static T SingleOrDefault<T>(
    this IEnumerable<T> source);

public static T SingleOrDefault<T>(
    this IEnumerable<T> source,
    Func<T, bool> predicate);
```

When the predicate function is specified it will be used against each element until the function returns **true**. The element that satisfies the predicate will be returned. If more than one element satisfies the predicate function, an exception will be thrown. In Listing 1-37 just one element (**9**) satisfies the predicate condition that the elements must be greater than 8.

Listing 1-37. An Example of Single with a Predicate Condition

```
int[] numbers = {1, 2, 3, 4, 5, 6, 7, 8, 9};
var query = numbers.Single(n => n > 8);
ObjectDumper.Write(query);
```

Using the **Single** method, if no element satisfies the predicate condition, an exception is thrown. Using the **SingleOrDefault** method (see Listing 1-38) either a **null** or **zero** value is returned when no element satisfies the predicate function. The difference between the **null** and **zero** value depends on the source type: **null** for reference types (i.e., **strings**) and **zero** for value types (i.e., **integers**).

Listing 1-38. The SingleOrDefault Method in Action

```
int[] numbers = {1, 2, 3, 4, 5, 6, 7, 8, 9};
var query = numbers.SingleOrDefault(n => n > 9);
ObjectDumper.Write(query);
```

Since no numeric element is greater than nine, a **zero** value will be returned.

ElementAt and ElementAtOrDefault

These methods return an element from the sequence at the specified zero-based index.

```
public static T ElementAt<T>(
    this IEnumerable<T> source,
    int index);
```

```
public static T ElementAtOrDefault<T>(
    this IEnumerable<T> source,
    int index);
```

When the code processes the query expression the method checks if the sequence implements the IList<T> type. If so the method uses the IList<T> implementation to obtain the element; otherwise the sequence will be enumerated until the index is reached.

Listing 1-39 uses ElementAt to retrieve the number 5 from the sequence.

Listing 1-39. Using ElementAt to Retrieve the Fifth Element

```
int[] numbers = {1, 2, 3, 4, 5, 6, 7, 8, 9};
var query = numbers.ElementAt(4);
ObjectDumper.Write(query);
```

When an invalid index is specified (i.e., an index less than zero) an exception of type ArgumentNullException is thrown. On the other hand, when using the ElementAtOrDefault method either a null or zero value will be returned (see Listing 1-40).

Listing 1-40. ElementAtOrDefault in Action

```
int[] numbers = {1, 2, 3, 4, 5, 6, 7, 8, 9};
var query = numbers.ElementAtOrDefault(9);
ObjectDumper.Write(query);
```

Since the tenth element is out of range the zero default value is returned.

DefaultIfEmpty

This operator replaces an empty element with a default element in a sequence, as in the following examples.

```
public static IEnumerable<T> DefaultIfEmpty<T>(
    this IEnumerable<T> source);
```

```
public static IEnumerable<T> DefaultIfEmpty<T>(
    this IEnumerable<T> source,
    T defaultValue);
```

If no default value parameter is specified, a `null` element will be yielded. This method is useful to produce left outer joins. See Listing 1-19 for a code-snippet sample.

Generation Operators

There are three generation operators: `Range`, `Repeat`, and `Empty`.

Empty

This operator returns an empty sequence of the specified type.

```
public static IEnumerable<T> Empty<T>();
```

When the `IEnumerable<T>` returned by the `Empty<T>` method is enumerated it yields nothing. Listing 1-41 shows how to produce an empty `Person` sequence:

Listing 1-41. An Empty Person Sequence Produced by the Empty<T> Method

```
IEnumerable<Person> p = Sequence.Empty<Person>();
ObjectDumper.Write(p);
```

The `p` variable contains no values, so the `Write()` method will not prompt any information.

Range

This operator produces a range of numeric values.

```
public static IEnumerable<int> Range(
    int start,
    int count);
```

When the `IEnumerable<int>` type is enumerated it produces a sequence of `count` elements starting from the `start` parameter value. In Listing 1-42 a sequence of ten numbers will be generated.

Listing 1-42. A Numeric Sequence from 1 to 10 Is Generated

```
ObjectDumper.Write(Sequence.Range(1, 10));
```

Repeat

This operator produces a sequence by repeating a value a given number of times.

```
public static IEnumerable<T> Repeat<T>(
    T element, int count);
```

The T element parameter will be generated the number of times indicated by the count parameter. In Listing 1-43 the first element of the Person sequence (people) is repeated ten times.

Listing 1-43. The Repeat Method in Action

```
List<Person> people = new List<Person> {
    new Person { ID = 1,
                IDRole = 1,
                LastName = "Anderson",
                FirstName = "Brad"},
    new Person { ID = 2,
                IDRole = 2,
                LastName = "Gray",
                FirstName = "Tom"},
    new Person { ID = 3,
                IDRole = 2,
                LastName = "Grant",
                FirstName = "Mary"},
    new Person { ID = 4,
                IDRole = 3,
                LastName = "Cops",
                FirstName = "Gary"}};

IEnumerable<Person> p = Sequence.Repeat(people[0], 10);

ObjectDumper.Write(p);
```

Figure 1-26 shows the output for the Listing 1-43.

Figure 1-26. The output of Listing 1-43

```
C:\WINDOWS\system32\cmd.exe                                              - □ ×
ID=1        IDRole=1        LastName=Anderson        FirstName=Brad
ID=1        IDRole=1        LastName=Anderson        FirstName=Brad
ID=1        IDRole=1        LastName=Anderson        FirstName=Brad
ID=1        IDRole=1        LastName=Anderson        FirstName=Brad
ID=1        IDRole=1        LastName=Anderson        FirstName=Brad
ID=1        IDRole=1        LastName=Anderson        FirstName=Brad
ID=1        IDRole=1        LastName=Anderson        FirstName=Brad
ID=1        IDRole=1        LastName=Anderson        FirstName=Brad
ID=1        IDRole=1        LastName=Anderson        FirstName=Brad
ID=1        IDRole=1        LastName=Anderson        FirstName=Brad
Press any key to continue . . . _
```

Quantifier Operators

There are three quantifiers: All, Any, and Contains.

All

This operator uses the predicate function against the elements of a sequence and returns **true** if all of them satisfy the predicate condition. Let's see the method's prototype:

```
public static bool All<T>(
    this IEnumerable<T> source,
    Func<T, bool> predicate);
```

The source sequence is enumerated and each element is used against the predicated function condition. If all of them satisfy the predicate condition then a **true** value is returned. Listing 1-44 uses the predicate to understand if all of sequence's elements are even. The output is Yes, they are.

Listing 1-44. Using the All method to Find Out If All of a Sequence's Elements Are Even

```
int[] numbers = { 2, 6, 24, 56, 102 };
Console.WriteLine("Are those all even numbers?");
ObjectDumper.Write(
    numbers.All(e => e % 2 == 0) ?
        "Yes, they are" : "No, they aren't");
```

Any

This operator searches a sequence for elements that satisfy the specified condition.

```
public static bool Any<T>(
    this IEnumerable<T> source);

public static bool Any<T>(
    this IEnumerable<T> source,
    Func<T, bool> predicate);
```

The predicate function is checked against each element of the source sequence, and stops as soon as the condition is satisfied. When the predicate parameter is not specified, the method returns a **true** value if the sequence is not empty. Listing 1-45 uses the predicate to understand if at least one element of the numeric sequence is odd. The output is `No, there isn't.`

Listing 1-45. Using the Any Method to Search for an Odd Numeric Value

```
int[] numbers = { 2, 6, 24, 56, 102 };
Console.WriteLine("Is there at least oneodd number?");
ObjectDumper.Write(
    numbers.Any(e => e % 2 == 1) ?
        "Yes, there is" : "No, there isn't");
```

Contains

This operator looks for a specified type within the sequence and returns true when the element is found.

```
public static bool Contains<T>(
    this IEnumerable<T> source,
    T value);
```

If the source sequence implements the ICollection<T> type then its Contains method will be used to search for the specified value. Otherwise the source sequence will be enumerated and each element will be compared to the value parameter until the element is found or the enumeration is over. A true value is returned when the element is found. If no element is found, a false value is returned. Listing 1-46 searches for and finds the number 102 within the sequence, so the output is Yes, there is.

Listing 1-46. The Contains Method Searches for the Specified Value in the Sequence.

```
int[] numbers = { 2, 6, 24, 56, 102 };
Console.WriteLine("Is there the number 102?");
ObjectDumper.Write(numbers.Contains(102) ?
    "Yes, there is" : "No, there isn't");
```

Equality Operator

There is one equality operator: SequenceEqual.

SequenceEqual

This operator compares two sequences and returns true when their elements are equal.

```
public static bool SequenceEqual<T>(
    this IEnumerable<T> first,
    IEnumerable<T> second);
```

Under the hood the code uses the other version of the SequenceEqual method that accepts an IEqualityComparer parameter. This method allows us to provide either a standard comparer such as the one created from the EqualityComparer class or a customized one. The SequenceEqual method will return a true Boolean value if both sequences contain the same elements (see Listing 1-47.)

Listing 1-47. Using the SequenceEqual Method with Equal and Unequal Sequences

```
int[] sequence1 = { 1, 2, 3, 4, 5 };
int[] sequence2 = { 1, 2, 3, 4, 5 };
```

```
Console.WriteLine("Are those sequence equal?");

ObjectDumper.Write(sequence1.SequenceEqual(sequence2) ?
    "Yes, they are" : "No, they aren't");

int[] sequence3 = { 1, 2, 3, 4, 5 };
int[] sequence4 = { 5, 4, 3, 2, 1 };

Console.WriteLine("Are those sequence equal?");
ObjectDumper.Write(sequence3.SequenceEqual(sequence4) ?
    "Yes, they are" : "No, they aren't");
```

Listing 1-47 starts comparing two sequences, sequence1 and sequence2. It compares the first element (1) of the first sequence with the first element (1) of the second sequence. Since they are equal, the method moves on to the other elements. The two sequences are equal, so the final output will be Yes, they are.

The next two sequences are different because the first element of the fourth sequence (1) is not equal to the first element of the fifth sequence (5). A false value is returned immediately and the output of the code is No, they aren't.

Set Operators

There are four set operators: Distinct, Intersect, Union, and Except.

Distinct

This operator is similar to the DISTINCT keyword used in SQL; it eliminates duplicates from a sequence.

```
public static IEnumerable<T> Distinct<T>(
    this IEnumerable<T> source);
```

When the code processes the query it enumerates the element of the sequence, storing into an IEnumerable<T> type each element that has not been stored previously. In Listing 1-48 the Distinct operator selects unique values from the sequence. The output will be 1, 2, 3.

Listing 1-48. The Distinct Operator in Action

```
int[] numbers = {1, 1, 2, 3, 3};
ObjectDumper.Write(numbers.Distinct());
```

Intersect

This operator returns a sequence made by common elements of two different sequences.

```
public static IEnumerable<T> Intersect<T>(
    this IEnumerable<T> first,
    IEnumerable<T> second);
```

The first sequence is enumerated and compared to the second one. Only the common element will be collected and inserted into the IEnumerable<T> return type. In Listing 1-49 the Intersect method compares two numeric sequences and returns the common elements: 1 and 3.

Listing 1-49. The Intersect Method Used to Retrieve Common Elements in Two Sequences

```
int[] numbers = {1, 1, 2, 3, 3};
int[] numbers2 = {1, 3, 3, 4};
ObjectDumper.Write(numbers.Intersect(numbers2));
```

Union

This operator returns a new sequence formed by uniting the two different sequences.

```
public static IEnumerable<T> Union<T>(
    this IEnumerable<T> first,
    IEnumerable<T> second);
```

The first sequence is enumerated and distinct elements are stored into an IEnumerable<T> type. The second sequence is enumerated as well and the elements not stored previously are added to the IEnumerable<T> return type. In Listing 1-50 the Union operator returns an IEnumerable<int> type composed of distinct elements from the two numeric sequences: 1, 3, 2, and 4.

Listing 1-50. The Union Operator in Action

```
int[] numbers = {1, 1, 3, 3};
int[] numbers2 = {1, 2, 3, 4};
ObjectDumper.Write(numbers.Union(numbers2));
```

Note   The Union operator doesn't sort the numbers when it produces the IEnumerable<T> return type.

Except

This operator produces a new sequence composed of the elements of the first sequence not present in the second sequence.

```
public static IEnumerable<T> Except<T>(
    this IEnumerable<T> first,
    IEnumerable<T> second);
```

When the code processes the query expression it starts to enumerate the first sequence, storing its distinct elements in an IEnumerable<T> type. Then it enumerates the second sequence and removes the common elements into the IEnumerable<T> type stored previously. Finally, it returns the processed IEnumerable<T> type to the caller. The output for the example shown in Listing 1-51 is 2, 4.

Listing 1-51. The Except Method in Action

```
int[] numbers = {1, 2, 3, 4};
int[] numbers2 = {1, 1, 3, 3};
ObjectDumper.Write(numbers.Except(numbers2));
```

Conversion Operators

There are seven conversion operators: OfType, Cast, ToSequence, ToArray, ToList, ToDictionary, and ToLookup.

OfType

This operator produces a new IEnumerable<T> type composed of only the element of the specified type.

```
public static IEnumerable<T> OfType<T>(
    this IEnumerable source);
```

The operator enumerates the elements of the source sequence, searching for those whose type is equal to T. Only those elements will be inserted in the final IEnumerable<T> sequence that the OfType method returns. Listing 1-52 searches for the elements of double type in the sequence. The result is 2.0.

Listing 1-52. The OfType Searches for the Specified Type T in the Sequence.

```
object[] sequence = {1, "Hello", 2.0};
ObjectDumper.Write(sequence.OfType<double>());
```

Cast

This operator casts the elements of the sequence to a given type.

```
public static IEnumerable<T> Cast<T>(
    this IEnumerable source);
```

The operator enumerates the elements of the source sequence and casts its elements to the T type. Those new elements are collected into a new IEnumerable<T> type that will be returned. Listing 1-53 casts object type to double type. The output will be 1.0, 2.0, 3.0.

Listing 1-53. The Cast Operator in Action

```
object[] doubles = {1.0, 2.0, 3.0};
IEnumerable<double> d = doubles.Cast<double>();
ObjectDumper.Write(d);
```

ToSequence

This operator simply returns the typed sequence to a given IEnumerable<T> type.

```
public static IEnumerable<T> ToSequence<T>(
    this IEnumerable<T> source);
```

This operator has no effect on the source sequence other than changing the type to IEnumerable<T>. This could be useful to call a standard query expression when a type implements its own query-expression methods.

ToArray

This operator returns an array composed of the elements of the source sequence.

```
public static T[] ToArray<T>(
    this IEnumerable<T> source);
```

In Listing 1-54 the elements of the people sequence that have the LastName length equal to 4 are retrieved and inserted into a string array.

Listing 1-54 does not use the ObjectDumper's Write method; eliminating it allowed me to demonstrate more clearly that the result of the query has been converted into an array. The output is Gray, Cops.

Listing 1-54. The Query Result Is Inserted into an Array Using the ToArray Operator.

```
List<Person> people = new List<Person> {
    new Person { ID = 1,
                 IDRole = 1,
                 LastName = "Anderson",
                 FirstName = "Brad"},
    new Person { ID = 2,
                 IDRole = 2,
                 LastName = "Gray",
                 FirstName = "Tom"},
    new Person { ID = 3,
                 IDRole = 2,
                 LastName = "Grant",
                 FirstName = "Mary"},
    new Person { ID = 4,
                 IDRole = 3,
                 LastName = "Cops",
                 FirstName = "Gary"}};

var query = from p in people
            where p.LastName.Length == 4
            select p.LastName;

string[] names = query.ToArray();

for(int i=0; i<names.Length; i++)
    Console.WriteLine(names[i]);
```

ToList

This operator returns a `List<T>` type composed of the elements of the source sequence.

```
public static List<T> ToList<T>(
    this IEnumerable<T> source);
```

In Listing 1-55 the result of the query is converted into a `List<string>` type. The output of this code snippet is `Gray, Cops`.

Listing 1-55. The ToList Method in Action

```
var query = from p in people
            where p.LastName.Length == 4
            select p.LastName;

List<string> names = query.ToList<string>();
ObjectDumper.Write(names);
```

ToDictionary

This operator returns a `Dictionary<K, E>` type composed of the elements of a sequence.

```
public static Dictionary<K, T> ToDictionary<T, K>(
    this IEnumerable<T> source,
    Func<T, K> keySelector);

public static Dictionary<K, T> ToDictionary<T, K>(
    this IEnumerable<T> source,
    Func<T, K> keySelector,
    IEqualityComparer<K> comparer);

public static Dictionary<K, E> ToDictionary<T, K, E>(
    this IEnumerable<T> source,
    Func<T, K> keySelector,
    Func<T, E> elementSelector);

public static Dictionary<K, E> ToDictionary<T, K, E>(
    this IEnumerable<T> source,
    Func<T, K> keySelector,
    Func<T, E> elementSelector,
    IEqualityComparer<K> comparer);
```

The prototype with both `keySelector` and `elementSelector` parameters is used to specify the elements of the sequence promoted to be the dictionary's key and value, respectively. When the `elementSelector` parameter is omitted the value will be the element itself. Finally, the prototype with the `comparer` parameter allows us to define a custom comparer function used during the `Dictionary<K, E>` type construction.

In Listing 1-56 .NET Reflection and LINQ are used to retrieve the int type's methods, which will be inserted into a Dictionary<string, int> type.

Listing 1-56. Using ToDictionary() to Retrieve a Dictionary<string, int> Type

```
var q = from m in typeof(int).GetMethods()
        group m by m.Name into gb
        select gb;

Dictionary<string, int> d =
    q.ToDictionary(k => k.Key, k => k.Count());
```

The query groups the methods of the int type. The ToDictionary() method is used to retrieve a dictionary with keys equal to the methods' name, and values equal to the methods' overloads number.

ToLookup

This operator returns a Lookup<K, T> type composed of elements from the source sequence.

```
public static Lookup<K, T> ToLookup<T, K>(
    this IEnumerable<T> source,
    Func<T, K> keySelector);

public static Lookup<K, T> ToLookup<T, K>(
    this IEnumerable<T> source,
    Func<T, K> keySelector,
    IEqualityComparer<K> comparer);

public static Lookup<K, E> ToLookup<T, K, E>(
    this IEnumerable<T> source,
    Func<T, K> keySelector,
    Func<T, E> elementSelector);

public static Lookup<K, E> ToLookup<T, K, E>(
    this IEnumerable<T> source,
    Func<T, K> keySelector,
    Func<T, E> elementSelector,
    IEqualityComparer<K> comparer);
```

```
public class Lookup<K, T> : IEnumerable<IGrouping<K, T>>
{
    public int Count { get; }
    public IEnumerable<T> this[K key] { get; }
    public bool Contains(K key);
    public IEnumerator<IGrouping<K, T>> GetEnumerator();
}
```

This new Lookup<K, T> type differs from Dictionary<K, E> type in the implementation of the type itself. The former allows us to associate a key with a sequence of values. The latter allows us to associate a key with a single value.

The prototype with both keySelector and elementSelector parameters is used to specify the elements of the sequence promoted to be the lookup's key and value, respectively. When the elementSelector parameter is omitted the value will be the element itself. Finally, the prototype with the comparer parameter allows us to define a custom comparer function used during the Lookup<K, T> type construction.

Listing 1-57 creates a Lookup<string, Salary> type whose key is equal to the Year element of the salaries sequence; the related value is the salary element itself.

Listing 1-57. The ToLookup Method Converts the Query Expression Result into a Lookup<string, Salary> Type.

```
List<Person> people = new List<Person> {
    new Person { ID = 1,
                 IDRole = 1,
                 LastName = "Anderson",
                 FirstName = "Brad"},
    new Person { ID = 2,
                 IDRole = 2,
                 LastName = "Gray",
                 FirstName = "Tom"},
    new Person { ID = 3,
                 IDRole = 2,
                 LastName = "Grant",
```

```
                    FirstName = "Mary"},
        new Person { ID = 4,
                    IDRole = 3,
                    LastName = "Cops",
                    FirstName = "Gary"}};

List<Salary> salaries = new List<Salary> {
    new Salary { IDPerson = 1, Year = 2004, SalaryYear = 10000.00 },
    new Salary { IDPerson = 1, Year = 2005, SalaryYear = 15000.00 }};

IEnumerable<Salary> q = from p in people
                       where p.ID == 1
                       from s in salaries
                       where s.IDPerson == p.ID
                       select s;

ILookup<string, Salary> d =
    q.ToLookup(k => k.Year.ToString(), k => k);
```

Summary

This long chapter covered the two main parts of LINQ to Objects.

First you examined the new C# 3.0 features to support LINQ. You saw how extension methods extend existing .NET types with new methods. You saw how lambda expressions improve code readability and help us write anonymous methods. You also saw other new features, such as anonymous types and expression trees.

Then you examined all the standard query operators and saw them in code examples to understand their functionality.

The next chapter covers LINQ to SQL, which is dedicated to querying information from relational databases such as Microsoft SQL Server. The query expression syntax you learned in this chapter is also used to query databases.

Chapter 2: LINQ to ADO.NET

This chapter covers the following:

Mapping LINQ to databases. Classes, properties, and attributes tell LINQ about database tables.

The DataContext class. This class supports LINQ's ORM functionality.

Advanced features. LINQ to SQL supports advanced database features such as transactions, optimist concurrency, stored procedure calls, and more.

LINQ to SQL in Visual Studio. Support for LINQ to SQL, including IntelliSense and debugging, are added to Visual Studio when LINQ is installed.

LINQ to DataSet. LINQ to SQL is integrated into ADO.NET, specifically with DataSet objects.

Introduction

In Chapter 1 we focused on the standard query operators, looking closely at each method for querying and modifying objects. You now know everything needed to query any data source. Whether data sources are in-memory objects, relational databases, or XML, we use the same uniform syntax to query them. An object is queryable as long as it implements the IQueryable<T> or IEnumerable<T> interface.

LINQ to SQL implements the IQueryable<T> interface to convert query expressions into Expression trees, which it transforms into SQL statements.

Results are stored using a basic ORM model, so rows are placed in objects created in our code. The LINQ to SQL run-time infrastructure can track each change to our objects. To persist changes, we call a method, and every tracked change will be propagated to the database.

LINQ to SQL is compatible with ADO.NET 2.0 classes such as `Connection` and `DataSet`. You can easily integrate LINQ to SQL with existing ADO.NET programs; hence this chapter's title.

Database Interaction

LINQ to SQL introduces LINQ functionality for Microsoft SQL Server 2000 and 2005. Thanks to the `IQueryable<T>` interface, it's theoretically possible to create providers for other databases. Although it's not in the scope of this book, see articles from Matt Warren at his blog site for more information: `http://blogs.msdn.com/mattwar/default.aspx`.

LINQ to SQL defines new C# attributes, properties, and classes to let us interact with SQL Server databases by mapping database objects to objects in our programs. Three basic steps are required:

1. Create classes for the tables in the database that you want to use, decorating them with appropriate LINQ attributes. These classes are usually called *entities*.

2. Decorate the fields and properties in these classes so LINQ can use them and knows how to use them.

3. Create a `DataContext` object to mediate between the database tables and the classes that map to them.

The next three sections provide examples of each step.

Mapping a Class to a Database Table

Mapping a class to a database table allows us to use LINQ against the table. The `Table` attribute, defined in the `System.Data.Linq` namespace, informs LINQ about how to map a class to a database table.

The following code simply declares a new public class named Person and associates it with the Person database table.

```
[Table(Name="Person")]
public class Person
```

The Table attribute's Name property is optional. LINQ uses the class name as the default table name.

Mapping Fields and Properties to Table Columns

Mapping fields and properties to table columns makes the columns available to LINQ. Figure 2-1 shows the Person table's structure. We want to make all the columns available to LINQ as properties of the Person class. Note that the first column is the primary key. It's also an IDENTITY column, so SQL Server automatically sets its value.

Figure 2-1. The Person table's structure

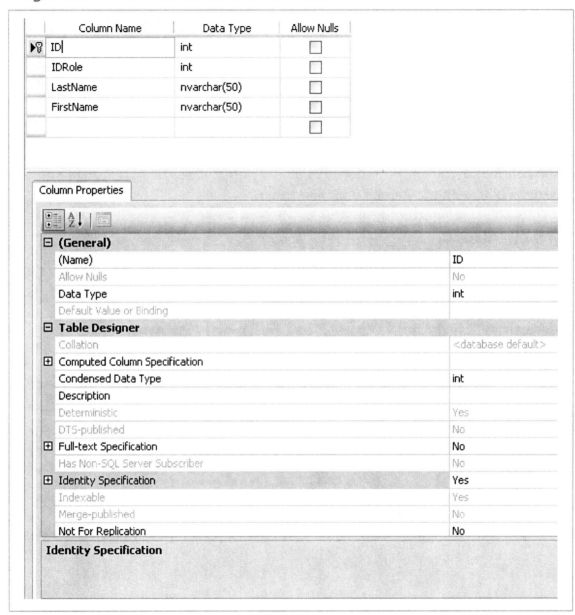

For each column we want to use with LINQ, we need to declare a property and decorate it with the Column attribute. Since we're using properties, we also declare private fields for the underlying data. For the first column, ID, we declare a field, _ID, and a property, ID.

```
[Table(Name="Person")]
public class Person
{
    private int _ID;

    [Column(Name="ID", Storage="_ID", DbType="int NOT NULL IDENTITY",
            IsPrimaryKey=true, IsDbGenerated=true)]
    public int ID
    {
        get { return _ID; }
        set { _ID = value; }
    }
}
```

The Column attribute has 11 properties (see Table 2-1), all of which are optional. We've used five of them. Name specifies the column name. DBType specifies not only the column's data type (int) but also that it's not nullable and is an IDENTITY column. The IsPrimaryKey property indicates that the column is part of the table's primary key. IsDbGenerated indicates that the column's value is generated by the database (which is true for all IDENTITY columns).

By default, LINQ uses a property's set and get accessors, but we can override this with the Storage property. For example, if we add the Storage property to the Column attribute for ID as follows, LINQ will use the underlying private field, _ID, instead of the accessors.

```
[Column(Name="ID", Storage="_ID", DbType="int NOT NULL IDENTITY",
        Id=true, IsDbGenerated=true)]
public int ID
{
    get { return _ID; }
    set { _ID = value; }
}
}
```

Now declare the private fields and public properties for the rest of the columns. The full class code is in Listing 2-1.

Listing 2-1. The Person Class Smapped to the Person Table in the People Database

```
[Table(Name="Person")]
public class Person
{
    private int _ID;
    private int _IDRole;
    private string _lastName;
    private string _firstName;

    [Column(Name="ID", Storage="_ID", DbType="int NOT NULL IDENTITY",
            IsPrimaryKey=true, IsDbGenerated=true)]
    public int ID
    {
        get { return _ID; }
        set { _ID = value; }
    }
}

    [Column(Name="IDRole", Storage="_IDRole", DbType="int NOT NULL")]
    public int IDRole
    {
        get { return _IDRole; }
        set { _IDRole = value; }
    }

    [Column(Name="LastName", Storage="_lastName",
      DbType="nvarchar NOT NULL")]
    public string LastName
    {
        get { return _lastName; }
        set { _lastName = value; }
    }
```

```
[Column(Name="FirstName", Storage="_firstName",
  DbType="nvarchar NOT NULL")]
public string FirstName
{
    get { return _firstName; }
    set { _firstName = value; }
}

}
```

Table 2-1. *Column-Attribute Properties*

PROPERTY	DESCRIPTION
AutoSync	Specifies if the column is automatically synchronized from the value generated by the database on insert or update commands. Valid values for this tag are Default, Always, Never, OnInsert, and OnUpdate.
CanBeNull	A Boolean value that indicates if the column can contain null values (true) or not (false).
DbType	Specifies the column's data type in the database. If you omit this property, LINQ will infer the type from the class member. This property is mandatory only if you want to use the CreateDatabase method to create a new database instance.
Expression	Defines the column as a computed column. Using this attribute you can define the formula used to compute the result.
IsDbGenerated	Identifies a column whose value is generated by the database. Usually used in conjunction with primary key columns defined with the IDENTITY property.

Table 2-1. continued

PROPERTY	DESCRIPTION
IsDiscriminator	Indicates that the member holds the discriminator value for an inheritance hierarchy.
IsPrimaryKey	Specifies that a column is part of a table's primary (or unique) key. LINQ currently works only with tables that have primary (or unique) keys.
IsVersion	Indicates the member is a database timestamp or version number.
Name	Specifies the column's name in the database. Defaults to the member name.
Storage	Specifies the name of the private field underlying a property. LINQ will bypass the property's get and set accessors and use the field instead.
UpdateCheck	Specifies how LINQ detects optimistic concurrency conflicts. The possible values are Always, Never, and WhenChanged. If no member is marked with IsVersion=true, all members participate in detection unless explicitly specified otherwise.

Creating a Data Context

A *data context* is an object of type System.Data.Linq.DataContext. It supports database retrieval and update for objects known to LINQ. It handles the database connection and implements the SQO for database access. To use tables in LINQ, they must not only be mapped but must also be available in a data context. You can make them available in two ways.

One way is to create a data context and then use it to create an object that LINQ can use as a table. For example, the two lines

```
DataContext PeopleDataContext = new DataContext(connString);
Table<Person> People = PeopleDataContext.GetTable<Person>();
```

create a data context, `PeopleDataContext`, and a `Table` collection, `People` (for the `Person` database table), available in that context.

A new generic collection class, `Table<T>`, in the `System.Data.Linq` namespace, is used to represent database tables. We used the data context's `GetTable<T>` method to create a `People` object of type `Table<Person>` in the `PeopleDataContext` context. The argument to the `DataContext` constructor is the same thing you provide an ADO.NET connection. Here is an example:

```
String connString = @"
    Data Source=.;
    Initial Catalog=People;
    Integrated Security=True
";
```

The result is that our database is known to LINQ as `PeopleDataContext` and the `Person` table is known as `People`.

Note　　The `Table<T>` generic collection type implements `IEnumerable<T>` and `IQueryable<T>` as well as `ITable`, which implements both `IEnumerable` and `IQueryable`.

The other—and recommended—way is to use a *strongly-typed data context*, like the following:

```
public partial class PeopleDataContext : DataContext
{
    public Table<Person> People;

    public PeopleDataContext(String connString) : base(connString) {}
}
```

In this example we declare a class, `PeopleDataContext`, to represent the data context. The class has a field, `People`, for the database table `Person`.

The constructor calls the `DataContext` base constructor with the connection string.

To use the strongly typed context, we'd instantiate it before performing our first query, like this:

```
PeopleDataContext people = new PeopleDataContext(connString);
```

In this case our database is known to LINQ as `people` and the `Person` table is known as `People`.

We've now written all we need for LINQ to manage the `Person` database table as the `People` collection. Querying it will be similar to what we did in Chapter 1 to query in-memory objects.

Querying a Database with LINQ to SQL

The only difference in querying a database with respect to an in-memory object is that we need to instantiate our data context before our first query. In Listing 2-2, the first line of code in `Main()` does this.

Listing 2-2. The Main Class Containing the Code to Query the Database

```
class Program
{
    static void Main(string[] args)
    {
        PeopleDataContext people = new PeopleDataContext();

        var query =
            from p in people.People
            from s in people.Salaries
            where p.ID == s.ID
            select new { p.LastName, p.FirstName, s.Year, s.SalaryYear };

        foreach(var row in query)
        {
            Console.WriteLine(
                "Name: {0}, {1} - Year: {2}",
                row.LastName,row.FirstName,row.Year);
```

```
            Console.WriteLine("Salary: {0}", row.SalaryYear);
        }
    }
}
```

The `DataContext` is the two-way channel by which LINQ queries the
database and the results are turned into objects. Figure 2-2 shows the
output of the code in Listing 2-2.

*Figure 2-2. The output is similar to examples from Chapter1 but this
time data is retrieved from a SQL Server database.*

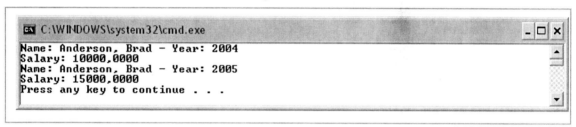

The `DataContext` class transforms the LINQ query into a SQL query. The
`Log` property of the `DataContext` class is an easy way to determine the SQL
query sent to the database. See the code snippet in Listing 2-3:

Listing 2-3. Displaying the SQL Query Sent by the Data Context

```
PeopleDataContext people = new PeopleDataContext();

people.Log = Console.Out;

var query =
    from p in people.People
    from s in people.Salaries
    where p.ID == s.ID
    select new { p.LastName, p.FirstName, s.Year, s.SalaryYear };

foreach(var row in query)
{
    Console.WriteLine(
        "Name: {0}, {1} - Year: {2}",
        row.LastName, row.FirstName, row.Year);
```

```
        Console.WriteLine("Salary: {0}", row.SalaryYear);
    }
```

The second line redirects the log to the console, as shown in Figure 2-3.

Figure 2-3. A SQL query sent by a data context

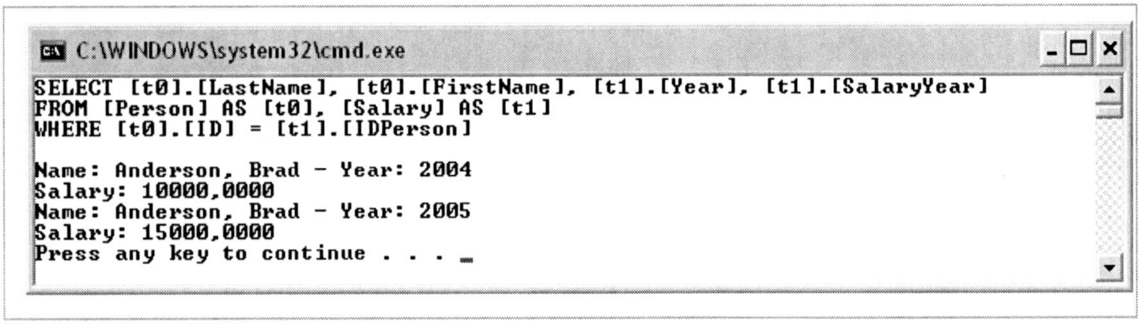

There is another way to see the SQL sent by LINQ. Use the GetCommand method of DataContext to see SELECT statements. The method requires the LINQ query as an argument and returns an object of DBCommand class. You can use its CommandText property to retrieve the SQL command used by LINQ to SQL to retrieve records from the database. On the other hand, the GetChangeSet method is used for INSERT, UPDATE, and DELETE statements. It returns an object of ChangeSet class that contains Inserts, Updates, and Deletes properties. They give access to a list of objects that is changed after an object associated with a database table is modified. Listing 2-4 shows these two methods in action.

Listing 2-4. Using GetQueryText and GetChangeText Methods to View SQL Statements

```
PeopleDataContext people = new PeopleDataContext();

var query =
    from p in people.People
    from s in people.Salaries
    where p.ID == s.ID
    select new { p.LastName, p.FirstName, s.Year, s.SalaryYear };
```

```
Console.WriteLine(
    people.GetCommand(query).CommandText);
Console.WriteLine();

foreach(var row in query)
{
    Console.WriteLine(
        "Name: {0}, {1} - Year: {2}",
        row.LastName, row.FirstName, row.Year);
    Console.WriteLine("Salary: {0}", row.SalaryYear);
}

Person person = new Person();
person.IDRole = 1;
person.FirstName = "From";
person.LastName = "Code";

people.People. InsertOnSubmit (person);

Console.WriteLine();
Console.WriteLine(people.GetChangeSet().ToString());
```

As you can see from the output shown in Figure 2-4, the ChangeSet object contains an *inserted* object. Using the Inserts property you can access to the new Person object added to the People collection.

Figure 2-4. Two other ways to retrieve the SQL statements built by LINQ

```
C:\WINDOWS\system32\cmd.exe                                        _ □ ×
SELECT [t0].[LastName], [t0].[FirstName], [t1].[Year], [t1].[SalaryYear]
FROM [dbo].[Person] AS [t0], [dbo].[Salary] AS [t1]
WHERE [t0].[ID] = [t1].[IDPerson]

Name: Anderson, Brad - Year: 2004
Salary: 10000.0000
Name: Anderson, Brad - Year: 2005
Salary: 15000.0000

{Inserts: 1, Deletes: 0, Updates: 0}
Press any key to continue . . .
```

Adding, Modifying, and Deleting Rows

As you can see in Listing 2-4, adding a new row consists of creating an object of a class that maps to a table, setting its values, and calling the InsertOnSubmit method on the appropriate Table<T> instance.

This is a classic object-oriented approach—adding an object to a collection—but this time you're adding a row to a database table! You don't write any SQL; everything is handled transparently by the data context. However, nothing happens in the database until you call the SubmitChanges method shown in Listing 2-5.

Listing 2-5. The SubmitChanges Method Propagates Changes to the Database.

```
PeopleDataContext people = new PeopleDataContext();

Person person = new Person();
person.IDRole = 1;
person.FirstName = "From";
person.LastName = "Code";
people.People.InsertOnSubmit(person);

people.SubmitChanges();

var query =
    from p in people.People
    select p;

foreach(var row in query)
{
    Console.WriteLine(
```

```
                    "Name: {0}, {1}", row.LastName, row.FirstName);
        }
```

After the `InsertOnSubmit` method has modified the `Person` table with a new row, the `SubmitChanges` method will contact the database and will execute the related SQL statement. Also, the method will be able to substitute the generic `@p0`, `@p1`, and `@p2` placeholders with the related value contained in the object. The output in Figure 2-5 shows that a new row has been added into the database.

Figure 2-5. A new row has been added from the code.

Let's learn to modify and delete rows. To modify a row, we first have to retrieve the row and change the values, as in Listing 2-6.

Listing 2-6. Modifying a Row with LINQ to SQL

```
PeopleDataContext people = new PeopleDataContext();

people.Log = Console.Out;

var person = people.People.Single(p => p.ID == 5);

person.FirstName = "Name";
person.LastName = "Modified";

people.SubmitChanges();
```

In the code snippet, using the `Single` method we retrieve the unique row whose `ID` is equal to 5. Then we change some attributes and call `SubmitChanges()` to update the database table. Figure 2-6 shows the SQL generated by LINQ.

Figure 2-6. The UPDATE statement built by the LINQ to SQL

```
C:\WINDOWS\system32\cmd.exe                                    _ | □ | ×
SELECT [t0].[ID], [t0].[IDRole], [t0].[LastName], [t0].[FirstName]
FROM [dbo].[Person] AS [t0]
WHERE [t0].[ID] = @p0
-- @p0: Input Int (Size = 0; Prec = 0; Scale = 0) [5]
-- Context: SqlProvider(Sql2005) Model: AttributedMetaModel Build: 3.5.21022.8

UPDATE [dbo].[Person]
SET [LastName] = @p4, [FirstName] = @p5
WHERE ([ID] = @p0) AND ([IDRole] = @p1) AND ([LastName] = @p2) AND ([FirstName]
= @p3)
-- @p0: Input Int (Size = 0; Prec = 0; Scale = 0) [5]
-- @p1: Input Int (Size = 0; Prec = 0; Scale = 0) [1]
-- @p2: Input NVarChar (Size = 4; Prec = 0; Scale = 0) [Code]
-- @p3: Input NVarChar (Size = 4; Prec = 0; Scale = 0) [From]
-- @p4: Input NVarChar (Size = 8; Prec = 0; Scale = 0) [Modified]
-- @p5: Input NVarChar (Size = 4; Prec = 0; Scale = 0) [Name]
-- Context: SqlProvider(Sql2005) Model: AttributedMetaModel Build: 3.5.21022.8

Press any key to continue . . .
```

As you can see, LINQ produces an UPDATE statement containing only the columns changed in the code. The first SELECT demonstrates that the Single method searches for the Person with an ID equal to 5.

Deleting a row is an easier process but it also involves a round trip to the database to first retrieve the row. We can use the Remove method of the DataContext class, and specify the object previously retrieved from a query. Listing 2-7 shows the code.

Listing 2-7. Using the Remove() Method to Delete a Row from the Database

```csharp
PeopleDataContext people = new PeopleDataContext();

people.Log = Console.Out;

// Select the record to remove
var person = from p in people.People
             where p.ID == 5
             select p;
```

```
people.People.DeleteOnSubmit(person.Single<Person>());

people.SubmitChanges();
```

The code retrieves a new `Person` object using the `Single<T>` generic method
to retrieve only one record. Finally, the object is passed to the
`DeleteOnSubmit` method and the changes are submitted with the
`SubmitChanges()` method call.

DataContext: Advanced Features

We've focused our attention on the basic features provided by LINQ to
SQL (in the `System.Data.Linq.dll` assembly). Data contexts have even
more features. In the next sections you'll see how to define relationships
between entities, and the benefits of doing that.

Defining Relationships Between Entities

The first feature we'll look at regards relationships between tables. A
relational database such as Microsoft SQL Server provides the capability to
define a relationship between two tables using primary and foreign keys.
For example, a table containing a list of orders could have a foreign key
pointing to a customers table. Using this relationship we can easily retrieve
all the orders made by a specific customer. Moreover, we can define the
rules to apply to the rows of related tables when some action occurs. For
example, we can inform the database to remove every order row for a
customer when the related customer is removed.

The relationships between objects are defined in a different way. Usually a
class contains a collection of related objects from another class.

LINQ to SQL provides a relational-like way to define a relationship
between two entity classes. Thanks to new generic types such as
`EntitySet<T>` and `EntityRef<T>`, it's possible to define the class members
that are involved in relationships.

The steps to implement relationships between entity classes are as follows:

1. Add an EntitySet<T> private field in the parent entity class to collect the objects belonging to the child entity class.

2. Add the property that encapsulates the access to this private field. Additionally, we have to add the Association decoration to specify some properties, such as the relation name and the keys involved in the relation.

3. Add the initialization of this private field using its two-parameter constructor.

4. Add an EntityRef<T> private field in the child entity class to retrieve the instance of the parent entity object.

5. Add the property that encapsulates the access to this private field. Again, we have to add the Association attribute to the property.

6. Add the initialization of this private field using the default constructor.

In the People database, the Person table has a foreign key, IDRole, pointing to the primary key of the Role table. Using the LINQ to SQL Association attribute (in the System.Data.Linq namespace) with the Role and Person class definitions, we can specify this kind of relationship between these tables in our code. Let's apply these steps to the Role and Person classes. Listing 2-8 gives the code for the parent entity class, Role.

Listing 2-8. The Role Entity Class

```
[Table(Name="Role")]
public class Role
{
    private int _ID;
    private string _Description;
    private EntitySet<Person> _People;

    public Role() {
        _People = new EntitySet<Person>(
            new Action<Person>(Attach_Person),
            new Action<Person>(Detach_Person));
    }
```

```csharp
[Association(Name="FK_Person_Role",
    Storage="_People",
    OtherKey="IDRole")]
public EntitySet<Person> People
{
    get { return _People; }
    set { _People.Assign(value); }
}

private void Attach_Person(Person entity) {
    entity.Role = this;
}

private void Detach_Person(Person entity) {
    entity.Role = null;
}

[Column(Storage = "_ID", Name = "ID",
    DbType = "Int NOT NULL IDENTITY",
    IsPrimaryKey = true,
    IsDbGenerated = true,
    CanBeNull = false)]
public int ID
{
    get
    {
        return this._ID;
    }
}
[Column(Name="RoleDescription",
        Storage="_Description",
        DbType="nvarchar NOT NULL",
        CanBeNull = false)]
public string RoleDescription
{
    get { return _Description; }
    set { _Description = value; }
}
}
```

The Role entity class represents the parent table. That's why it has

```
private EntitySet<Person> _People;
```

which contains the People objects that belong to a role.

The Role class has to define a public property that encapsulates the access code to the EntitySet<Person> private field. Here is the code snippet for it:

```
[Association(Name="FK_Person_Role",
             Storage="_People",
             OtherKey="IDRole")]
public EntitySet<Person> People

public EntitySet<Person> People
{
    get { return _People; }
    set { _People.Assign(value); }
}
```

The Assign method of EntitySet<T> sets the new value in the collection so that the new object is monitored by LINQ to SQL and by its change-tracking service.

The Association attribute informs LINQ to SQL about the relationship name, the private field used to store the Person objects collection, and the foreign key in the related table. The Association attribute provides the ThisKey property too (see Table 2-2 for the full list of properties). It represents the parent-table key related to the OtherKey. In our example, ThisKey has been omitted because it coincides with the primary key and the LINQ to SQL is able to infer its name automatically.

Table 2-2. The Full List of the Association Attribute's Properties

PROPERTY	DESCRIPTION
DeleteOnNull	You can decide to delete child objects when their parent is deleted. This is set to true when the Cascade option in the DeleteRule of the relationship defined in SQL Server is specified.

DeleteRule	Specifies the delete behavior associated with the foreign key. For example, it is possible to add cascade records' deletions when using this property.
IsForeignKey	When set to `true` this property indicates that the column represents the foreign key.
IsUnique	When set to `true` this property indicates that there is a 1:1 relationship between entities.
Name	Identifies the name of the relation. Usually its value is the same as the name of the foreign key constraint relation name defined in the database. You have to specify it if you plan to use the `CreateDatabase()` method from the `DataContext` class to create a new database with this relation. You have to use the same name in the entity class that composes the relation with this one.
OtherKey	Identifies a list of parent entity class keys separated by commas. If the keys are not specified, LINQ to SQL infers them, and assumes they are equal to the primary keys defined in the parent entity class.
Storage	`Storage` contains the name of the private field defined in the class. When specifying this property, LINQ to SQL will use the class's field to access data instead of using the related `get` and `set` accessors.
ThisKey	Identifies a list of keys of this entity class, separated by commas. If the keys are not specified, LINQ to SQL assumes they are equal to the primary keys defined in this class.

The next step is to initialize the private field using the `Role` class constructor:

```
public Role() {
    _People = new EntitySet<Person>(
        new Action<Person>(Attach_Person),
        new Action<Person>(Detach_Person));
}
```

We pass two delegate methods to the EntitySet<T> constructor. The Attach_Person method will set the related Role object to the new Person object. The Detach_Person method will set to null the related Role object in the Person object:

```
private void Attach_Person(Person entity) {
    entity.Role = this;
}

private void Detach_Person(Person entity) {
    entity.Role = null;
}
```

In the child entity class related to the Person database table, we add a private EntityRef<Role> field so we'll be able to retrieve its role simply:

```
Console.WriteLine(person.Role.RoleDescription);
```

Next we have to add a public property containing the accessors to get and set the private field value. In accordance with the steps listed earlier, we have to use the Association attribute even with this public property. Here we should define the same name used in the earlier example because LINQ to SQL has to know that we are going to define the other side of the relation. Moreover, using the ThisKey property we can specify the column name of the child entity class related to the foreign key column of the database table.

Listing 2-9 shows how to modify the Person class to define the relationship with the Role class:

Listing 2-9. The Person Class Modified to Include the Relationship with the Role Class

```
[Table(Name="Person")]
public class Person
{
    private int _ID;
    private int _IDRole;
    private string _lastName;
    private string _firstName;

    public Person() {
        _Role = default(EntityRef<Role>);
    }

    [Column(Name="FirstName",
            Storage="_firstName",
            DbType="nvarchar NOT NULL",
            CanBeNull = false)]
    public string FirstName
    {
        get { return _firstName; }
        set { _firstName = value; }
    }

    [Column(Name="LastName",
            Storage="_lastName",
            DbType="nvarchar NOT NULL",
            CanBeNull = false)]
    public string LastName
    {
        get { return _lastName; }
        set { _lastName = value; }
    }

    [Column(Name="IDRole",
            Storage="_IDRole",
            DbType="int NOT NULL",
            CanBeNull = false)]
    public int IDRole
    {
        get { return _IDRole; }
        set { _IDRole = value; }
```

```csharp
    }

    [Column(Storage = "_ID",
Name = "ID",
DbType = "Int NOT NULL IDENTITY",
IsPrimaryKey = true,
CanBeNull = false)]
    public int ID
    {
        get
        {
            return this._ID;
        }
    }
    private EntityRef<Role> _Role;

    [Association(Name="FK_Person_Role",
                Storage="_Role",
                ThisKey="IDRole",
                OtherKey="ID",
                IsForeignKey=true)]
    public Role Role
    {
        get { return _Role.Entity; }
        set {
            Role previousValue = this._Role.Entity;
            if (((previousValue != value)
                        || (this._Role.HasLoadedOrAssignedValue == false)))
            {
                if ((previousValue != null))
                {
                    this._Role.Entity = null;
                    previousValue.People.Remove(this);
                }
                this._Role.Entity = value;
                if ((value != null))
                {
                    value.People.Add(this);
                    this._IDRole = value.ID;
                }
                else
                {
                    this._IDRole = default(int);
```

```
                }
              }
            }
          }
        }
```

The following class constructor uses the **default** keyword applied to a generic type to initialize its value:

```
public Person() {
    _Role = default(EntityRef<Role>);
}
```

The **default** keyword applied to a **struct** data type such as the **EntityRef<T>** initializes every single field within the **struct**, setting the reference data types to **null** and the numeric-value data types to zero.

In the **set** accessor we check if the value specified is different from the one within the **Entity** property of the **_Role** field or if the **_Role** field is still not been loaded or assigned. If so, we have to remove the old one before adding the new value. Finally, the **Person** object pointed by the **this** keyword is added to the **People** collection to maintain referential integrity:

```
public Role Role
{
    get { return _Role.Entity; }
    set {
        Role previousValue = this._Role.Entity;
        if (((previousValue != value)
                    || (this._Role.HasLoadedOrAssignedValue == false)))
        {
            if ((previousValue != null))
            {
                this._Role.Entity = null;
                previousValue.People.Remove(this);
            }
            this._Role.Entity = value;
            if ((value != null))
            {
                value.People.Add(this);
                this._IDRole = value.ID;
```

```
        }
        else
        {
            this._IDRole = default(int);
        }
    }
  }
}
```

Using Two Related Entity Classes

Now that we've defined the relationship between two entity classes we can use it to query and modify data.

The code in Listing 2-10 retrieves a single **Person** object and then uses its role.

Listing 2-10. Retrieving a Person and Using Its Role Property

```
PeopleDataContext people = new PeopleDataContext();

people.Log = Console.Out;

var query =
    from p in people.People
    where p.ID == 1
    select p;

foreach(var row in query)
{



    Console.WriteLine(
        "Full Name: {0} {1} Role: {2}",
        row.FirstName,
        row.LastName,
        row.Role.RoleDescription);
}
```

We don't need to the join the two tables to access the role. LINQ to SQL generates two SQL queries to retrieve both the **Person** and related **Role** data. See the two SQL statements in Figure 2-7.

Figure 2-7. The output of Listing 2-10

```
C:\WINDOWS\system32\cmd.exe                                    _ □ ×

SELECT [t0].[FirstName], [t0].[LastName], [t0].[IDRole], [t0].[ID]
FROM [Person] AS [t0]
WHERE [t0].[ID] = @p0

SELECT [t0].[ID], [t0].[RoleDescription]
FROM [Role] AS [t0]
WHERE [t0].[ID] = @p0

Full Name: Brad Anderson Role: Manager
Press any key to continue . . .
```

Note in Figure 2-7 that the @p0 parameter is used in both the queries. They are two different queries, so the @p0 parameter has different values. The @p0 parameter used in the first query is the value specified in the LINQ query. The @p0 parameter used in the second query is the value specified with the ThisKey property of the Association attribute used in the Role property decoration.

In Listing 2-11 we'll retrieve a role and then use its People property to add a new person.

Listing 2-11. Adding a New Person to the Database Starting from a Role

```
PeopleDataContext people = new PeopleDataContext();

people.Log = Console.Out;

Role role = people.Roles.Single(r => r.ID == 1);

Person person = new Person();
person.FirstName = "From";
person.LastName = "Relationship";
role.People.Add(person);

people.SubmitChanges();
```

Since there's a relationship between the two entity classes, we don't have to specify the IDRole for the Person object. It will be assigned by the

Attach_Person delegate function when a new Person object is added to the people collection of the Role entity class. Figure 2-8 shows the INSERT statement generated by LINQ to SQL. The last SELECT statement returns the new Person's ID so that the Person object in the code can be aligned with database-related record.

Figure 2-8. The INSERT statement generated by LINQ to SQL

```
C:\WINDOWS\system32\cmd.exe                                              _|□|×|
SELECT [t0].[ID], [t0].[RoleDescription]
FROM [Role] AS [t0]
WHERE [t0].[ID] = @p0
-- @p0: Input Int (Size = 0; Prec = 0; Scale = 0) [1]
-- Context: SqlProvider(Sql2005) Model: AttributedMetaModel Build: 3.5.21022.8

INSERT INTO [dbo].[Person]([IDRole], [LastName], [FirstName])
VALUES (@p0, @p1, @p2)

SELECT CONVERT(Int,SCOPE_IDENTITY()) AS [value]
-- @p0: Input Int (Size = 0; Prec = 0; Scale = 0) [1]
-- @p1: Input NVarChar (Size = 12; Prec = 0; Scale = 0) [Relationship]
-- @p2: Input NVarChar (Size = 4; Prec = 0; Scale = 0) [From]
-- Context: SqlProvider(Sql2005) Model: AttributedMetaModel Build: 3.5.21022.8

Press any key to continue . . .
```

Deleting a row and every row related to it is really simple when a relationship is defined between two entity classes. Listing 2-12 deletes a role and all its related Person records.

Listing 2-12. Deleting a Role and All of Its Related Person Records

```
PeopleDataContext people = new PeopleDataContext();

people.Log = Console.Out;

Role role = new Role();
role.RoleDescription = "Administrator";

Person person = new Person();
person.FirstName = "From";
person.LastName = "Code";

role.People.Add(person);
```

```
people.Roles.InsertOnSubmit(role);

people.SubmitChanges();

Role admin = people.Roles.Single(r => r.ID == role.ID);
people.Roles.DeleteOnSubmit(admin);
people.SubmitChanges();
```

It creates a new role as follows:

```
Role role = new Role();
role.RoleDescription = "Administrator";
```

then adds a new person to it:

```
Person person = new Person();
person.FirstName = "From";
person.LastName = "Code";

role.People.Add(person);
people.Roles.InsertOnSubmit(role);
```

The code uses the new role's identifier to retrieve the new row added to the database:

```
Role admin = people.Roles.Single(r => r.ID == role.ID);
people.Roles.DeleteOnSubmit(admin);
people.SubmitChanges();
```

We have provided two delegate functions responding to the Add and the Remove events of the Person entity class. In the body of the Detach_Person delegate function we have set the Role value to null, raising a call to the set accessor of the Role property. It's in the body of Detach_Person that you will find the Remove() method of the Person row related to the role. The Remove() method applied by the parent class will call the Detach delegate function for each child row related to it. This process will be performed once for each Person object related to the Role object.

Note   The code works because there is a Delete Rule defined into the database set to Cascade for the foreign key relationships that relates the `Person` table to the `Role` table. On the other hand, you have to remove child records manually from the code before deleting the parent record.

Other LINQ to SQL Features

In this section we'll cover the following:

- Using SQLMetal to produce entity classes and associations automatically
- Using the `INotifyPropertyChanging` interface to communicate with LINQ about changes
- Using the optimistic concurrency and database transactions
- Using stored procedures
- Creating a database from a program

SQLMetal

LINQ to SQL has a command-line tool called SQLMetal that generates entity classes, properties, and associations automatically. Table 2-3 lists the SQLMetal options.

Table 2-3. SQLMetal Generation Tool Options

OPTION	DESCRIPTION
/server:<name>	Represents the Microsoft SQL Server server name to which it connects.
/database:<name>	Represents the Microsoft SQL Server database name to use to produce entity classes.

OPTION	DESCRIPTION
/user:<name>	Represents the user's name to use to connect to the database server.
/password:<name>	Represents the user's password to use to connect to the database server.
/conn:<connectionString>	Lets you specify a connection string to connect to the database.
/timeout:<value>	Lets you specify the timeout (in seconds) to use for each database command.
/views	Obtains the database views extraction.
/functions	Obtains the database user functions extraction.
/sprocs	Obtains the database stored procedures extraction.
/dbml:<filename>	Lets you specify a DBML filename that will contain the database metadata and some information about classes and properties.
/code:<filename>	Lets you specify the name of the file that will contain the entity classes and data context.
/map:<filename>	Obtains an external XML file with mapping attributes. The entities produced in the code will not contain class and property attributes' decorations because they have been included in the XML mapping file.

Table 2-3. continued

OPTION	DESCRIPTION
/language:<name>	There are two options: C# (the default) and VB. Use one of these options to produce a file in the specified language.
/namespace	Lets you specify the namespace that will contain the generated entity classes.
/context:<name>	You can specify the name of the class derived by the DataContext class.
/entitybase:<name>	You can indicate the name of the base entity class from which other entities will inherit.
/pluralize	Obtains entity class and property names with English plural.
/serialization:<param>	Generates serializable classes. Possible values are None and Unidirectional.
/provider:<name>	Lets you specify the name of the provider to use to connect to the database. Possible values are SQLCompact, SQL2000, or SQL2005.

The following command uses SQLMetal to generate the entity classes to access to the People database within a Microsoft SQL Server 2005 database using Windows Integrated Security:

```
sqlmetal /server:pc-ferracchiati /database:People /pluralize /code:People.cs
```

If you want to use SQL Server security you have to add two more options to the command, specifying username and password:

```
sqlmetal /server:pc-ferracchiati /database:People /user:sa
        /password:sapass /pluralize /code:People.cs
```

You can also generate entity classes simply by specifying a database's data (.MDF) file:

```
sqlmetal /pluralize /code:People.cs c:\data\people.mdf
```

The INotifyPropertyChanging Interface

By opening up the code produced by the SQLMetal tool, we can see some minor differences between it and the code we wrote. There are four types of constructor accepting different connection attributes, such as a connection string and an IDBConnection object, but the big difference is the use of the INotifyPropertyChanging and INotifyPropertyChanged:

```
[Table(Name="Person")]
public partial class Person : INotifyPropertyChanging, INotifyPropertyChanged
{

    private int _ID;
```

Both the INotifyPropertyChanging interface and the INotifyPropertyChanged interface are in the System.ComponentModel namespace. Both interfaces require two events:

```
public event PropertyChangedEventHandler PropertyChanging;
public event PropertyChangedEventHandler PropertyChanged;
```

They also require virtual methods to handle the interfaces:

```
protected virtual void SendPropertyChanging() {
  if ((this.PropertyChanging != null)) {
    this.PropertyChanging(this, emptyChangingEventArgs);
  }
}

protected virtual void SendPropertyChanged(string propertyName) {
  if ((this.PropertyChanged != null)) {
    this.PropertyChanged(this, new PropertyChangedEventArgs(propertyName));
  }
}
```

The emptyChangingEventArgs field is a private static class's field defined in the class as an object of the PropertyChangingEventArgs class created providing an empty string as parameter. In the generated code, each set accessor of a column calls two methods. The SendPropertyChanging method is called just before the variable is set to the provided value. The SendPropertyChanged method is called just after the variable is set.

```
[Column(Storage="_ID",
  AutoSync.OnInsert,
  DbType="Int NOT NULL IDENTITY",
  IsPrimaryKey=true,
  IsDbGenerated=true)]
public int ID {
  get {
    return this._ID;
  }
  set {
    if ((this._ID != value)) {
            this.OnIDChanging(value);
            this.SendPropertyChanging();
            this._ID = value;
            this.SendPropertyChanged("ID");
            this.OnIDChanged();
    }
  }
}
  }
}
```

Note   Since the column is the IDENTITY type, the SQLMetal adds the AutoSync attribute to refresh column's value when a new record is inserted.

The use of INotifyPropertyChanging and INotifyPropertyChanged is not mandatory. In fact, the code we wrote works very well. But these interfaces help LINQ change tracking. The SendPropertyChanging and SendPropertyChanged methods significantly improve change tracking because LINQ doesn't have to check changes manually. If you don't use these two interfaces and you don't inform LINQ about row changes, it will use two copies of the same object to understand if something is changed. There will be two objects representing each table, wasting memory and cycles when you call SubmitChanges().

Optimistic Concurrency and Database Transactions

What we have done to this point works well only if we are the only ones working on a set of data. If an application uses a LINQ query to retrieve data from a table already accessed by another user and then it tries to modify some rows, it could get an exception. This is because LINQ to SQL uses *optimistic concurrency*.

LINQ to SQL tracks changes to our objects after they are retrieved by a query and filled by a foreach statement or a call to a caching method such as ToList(). If another user has retrieved a row from the database and already changed its contents, when we try to submit our changes we'll get an exception. In fact, LINQ's change-tracking service discovers that the row has been changed from its original state (as of when we retrieved it) and raises the exception. To test the optimistic concurrency feature, write and execute the code in Listing 2-13.

Listing 2-13. Testing the Optimistic Concurrency Feature

```
PeopleDataContext people = new PeopleDataContext();

Person p = people.People.Single(person => person.ID == 1);

p.LastName = "Optimistic";
p.FirstName = "Concurrency";

Console.ReadLine();

people.SubmitChanges();
```

The code simply retrieves the Person row whose identifier is equal to 1, changes some attributes, and submits the changes after a key is pressed.

This allows us to execute another instance of the same application that retrieves the same row before we press a key in the other instance of the application. Pressing a key in the first application will modify the row, whereas pressing a key in the second application will cause the exception shown in Figure 2-9.

Figure 2-9. The exception thrown by LINQ when the optimistic concurrency is violated

```
C:\WINDOWS\system32\cmd.exe                                              _ |□| x|

Unhandled Exception: System.Data.Linq.ChangeConflictException: Row not found or
changed.
    at System.Data.Linq.ChangeProcessor.SubmitChanges(ConflictMode failureMode)
    at System.Data.Linq.DataContext.SubmitChanges(ConflictMode failureMode)
    at System.Data.Linq.DataContext.SubmitChanges()
    at LINQToSQL.Program.Main(String[] args) in C:\Documents and Settings\Adminis
trator\Desktop\LINQ_for_VisualC#_2005\Chapter02\LINQToSQL\LINQToSQL\Program.cs:l
ine 187
Press any key to continue . . .
```

Concurrency is managed by the DataContext class. When we call SubmitChanges(), the data context creates a local transaction using the ReadCommit isolation level; that is, using optimistic concurrency.

This is the default. When we decorate the properties of the entity classes we can indicate which of them participate in optimistic concurrency. Using the UpdateCheck property of the Column attribute we can specify Never and LINQ will ignore the column during concurrency checking.

```
[Column(Name="FirstName",
        Storage="_firstName",
        DbType="nvarchar NOT NULL",
        UpdateCheck=UpdateCheck.Never)]
public string FirstName
{
    get { return _firstName; }
    set { _firstName = value; }
}
```

```
[Column(Name="LastName",
        Storage="_lastName",
        DbType="nvarchar NOT NULL",
        UpdateCheck=UpdateCheck.Never)]
public string LastName
{
    get { return _lastName; }
    set { _lastName = value; }
}
```

After we modify the Person entity class as shown, the code in Listing 2-13 will work without exceptions because the two columns don't participate in optimistic concurrency checking.

Note   Before running the example in Listing 2-13 again, you have to change the record to put Anderson Brad as a person in the database. This is necessary because the SELECT executed by the Single method returns the current record that already owns the lastname and firstname values you will change using LINQ. In other words, optimistic concurrency values are already in the database and no UPDATE command will be executed if you specify the same values with LINQ. Obviously, you can change the code and provide different values to LastName and FirstName properties as well.

LINQ to SQL provides an advanced technique to manage update conflicts. When we call SubmitChanges(), we can specify a ConflictMode enum value to change the way optimistic concurrency is managed by LINQ.

Using ConflictMode.ContinueOnConflict the ChangeConflictException is filled with some attributes that we can use to personalize the way optimistic concurrency is managed. Using a **try** statement we can catch the ChangeConflictException and then use the ResolveAll() method provided by the ChangeConflicts property of the DataContext class to specify one of three values from the RefreshMode enumeration that in turn specify three different ways to resolve update conflicts:

KeepChanges: The old values contained in the object are refreshed with the new values changed by the other client. A new SubmitChanges() call is executed automatically and the current values within the object are used to update the row.

KeepCurrentValues: This rolls back each change made by the other client to the original database state. A new SubmitChanges() call is executed automatically and the current values within the object are used to update the row.

OverwriteCurrentValues: The object replaces its data with the new state of the row in the database.

The code in Listing 2-14 calls the ResolveAll method with KeepChanges after an optimistic concurrency exception has been detected.

Listing 2-14. A try Statement to Manage Optimistic Concurrency Conflict

```
PeopleDataContext people = new PeopleDataContext();

Person p = people.People.Single(person => person.ID == 1);

p.IDRole = 2;

try
{
    people.SubmitChanges(ConflictMode.ContinueOnConflict);
}
catch (ChangeConflictException cce)
{
    people.ChangeConflicts.ResolveAll(RefreshMode.KeepChanges);
}
```

Sometimes we need to lock a row until we've finished managing it. This can be done by using a transaction and the *pessimistic concurrency* feature.

.NET 2.0 provides the TransactionScope class in the System.Transactions namespace. A simple way to implement pessimistic concurrency is with a using statement. Within a using block we can instantiate a TransactionScope and, as the last operation, call its Complete() method (see Listing 2-15).

Listing 2-15. Implementing Pessimistic Concurrency with TransactionScope

```
PeopleDataContext people = new PeopleDataContext();

using (TransactionScope t = new TransactionScope())
{
    Person p = people.People.Single(person => person.ID == 1);

    p.LastName = "Pessimistic";
    p.FirstName = "Concurrency";

    Console.ReadLine();

    people.SubmitChanges();

    t.Complete();
}
```

We can test the pessimistic concurrency by executing two separate application instances (like in Listing 2-13). Both transactions attempt to lock the same row, and SQL Server decides which one (the "deadlock victim") to terminate (see Figure 2-10).

Figure 2-10. Pessimistic concurrency deadlock resolution

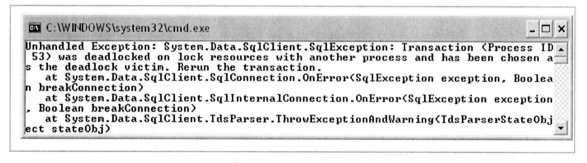

LINQ to SQL is able to integrate itself even with the old ADO.NET application code. We can use the `DataContext` class with `SqlTransaction` classes, but we'll have to do much more work to implement the local transaction. In the code snippet in Listing 2-16 a new `Role` is added to the related table using an ADO.NET local transaction.

Listing 2-16. Using an ADO.NET Local Transaction with LINQ to SQL

```
PeopleDataContext people = new PeopleDataContext();
people.Log = Console.Out;

Role r = new Role();
r.RoleDescription = "Integration with old ADO.NET apps";
people.Roles.InsertOnSubmit(r);

people.Connection.Open();
people.Transaction = people.Connection.BeginTransaction();

try
{
    people.SubmitChanges();
    people.Transaction.Commit();
}
catch (Exception ex)
{
    people.Transaction.Rollback();
    throw ex;
}
finally
{
    if (people.Connection.State == System.Data.ConnectionState.Open)
        people.Connection.Close();

    people.Transaction = null;
}
```

As you can see in Listing 2-16, we have to pay attention to some things, such as manually opening and closing the connection and calling `Commit()` or `Rollback()` (when everything is fine or something goes wrong, respectively).

Stored Procedures

LINQ to SQL automatically produces SQL statements to select rows, insert rows, and so on. We often prefer to use existing stored procedures or create new ones to access data and improve application performance. *Stored procedures* are SQL statement procedures that are precompiled and stored within the SQL Server database. When you call a stored procedure, the database server simply executes it without doing other operations such as checking SQL syntax within it. In many cases calling a stored procedure to retrieve rows works better than using dynamic SQL.

LINQ to SQL provides the ExecuteCommand method of the DataContext class to call stored procedures. This method has two parameters: the SQL command to execute and the collection of parameters that can be used in the SQL command.

Within the class inheriting from the DataContext we can add a method to call the ExecuteCommand() method that provides the stored procedure name and its parameters:

```
public void InsertRole(Role r)
{
this.ExecuteCommand("exec uspInsertRole @description={0}", r.RoleDescription);
}
```

The uspInsertRole stored procedure simply adds a new role, accepting its description as a parameter (Role's identifier is auto-incremented by the server since it is of the identity type). The ExecuteCommand() method will substitute each placeholder specified in the command with the related parameter contained in the collection.

Up to this point we have written all the necessary code to execute our stored procedure instead of executing the code generated by LINQ to SQL. In Listing 2-17 a new role is added to the related table and the Log property is used to show the code called by LINQ.

Listing 2-17. A New Role Is Added and the Stored Procedure Is Called Automatically.

```
PeopleDataContext people = new PeopleDataContext();
people.Log = Console.Out;

Role r = new Role();
r.RoleDescription = "By SP";
people.Roles.InsertOnSubmit(r);

people.SubmitChanges();
```

When you executing the code you will obtain the result shown in Figure 2-11, which displays how LINQ calls the stored procedure automatically.

Figure 2-11. The framework uses our stored procedure instead of generating the code to insert a new role.

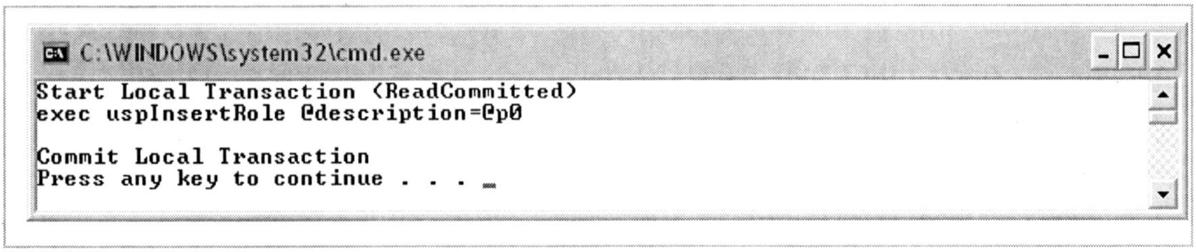

To update rows using a stored procedure we can specify an update method in the class that inherits from the `DataContext` class. The prototype of the update method is similar to the one used to insert a record, except using the Update word instead of the Insert word:

```
public void UpdateRole(Role newRole)
{
    int iRowsAffected = this.uspUpdateRole(
       newRole.ID, newRole.RoleDescription);

    if (iRowsAffected < 1)
       throw new ChangeConflictException();
}
```

Moreover, we have to check the return value of `uspUpdateRole()` because if it is less than 1 an optimistic concurrency error has occurred. In that case we must throw a new `ChangeConflictException` exception. The `uspUpdateRole()` method is responsible to call the stored procedure in the People database. Its internal code is similar to other methods you will see soon in a few pages.

Note   In order to retrieve the current number of affected rows after the stored procedure execution you have to add the `RETURN @@ROWCOUNT` instruction at the end of the stored procedure code.

Listing 2-18 shows the code that will call the update stored procedure automatically.

Listing 2-18. Updating a Role Calling a Stored Procedure Instead of Using the LINQ to SQL Update-Generated Statement

```
PeopleDataContext people = new PeopleDataContext();
people.Log = Console.Out;

Role r = people.Roles.Single(role => role.ID == 1);
r.RoleDescription = "By Update stored procedure";

people.SubmitChanges();
```

To delete a row by using a stored procedure we have to add a new method in the class that inherits from the `DataContext`:

```
public void DeleteRole(Role r)
{
    this.ExecuteCommand("exec uspDeleteRole @id={0}", r.ID);
}
```

In this way the code in Listing 2-19 will call a stored procedure to remove each role from the database.

```
PeopleDataContext people = new PeopleDataContext();
people.Log = Console.Out;

var query = people.Roles
            .Where(role =>
            role.RoleDescription == "By Update stored procedure ")
            .Select(role => role);

foreach (Role r in query)
    people.Roles.DeleteOnSubmit(r);

people.SubmitChanges();
```

Note   There is nothing magical about defining a method having a prefixed name and seeing that **DataContext** calls it automatically. This is a new C# 3.0 feature called *partial method*. You can use the **partial** keyword to define a method's prototype (having particular characteristics such as no return type). This method will be ignored by the compiler if you don't provide an implementation to the method, leaving just the partial method's prototype.

By using SQLMetal with the **/sprocs** option we can generate entity classes containing methods that have the same name as a stored procedure. Based on the syntax of the stored procedure, the generated code could return a single value or a collection of objects.

The simplest case is a stored procedure that computes scalar operations using the **COUNT** operator:

```
create procedure uspCountPerson
as
    declare @count int
    set @count = (select count(ID) from person)
    return @count
```

Executing the SQLMetal application with the /sprocs option, the generated
code will contain the following method:

```
[Function(Name="dbo.uspCountPerson")]
public int uspCountPerson() {
  IExecuteResults result =
    ExecuteMethodCall(this,
      ((MethodInfo)(MethodInfo.GetCurrentMethod())));
  return ((int)(result.ReturnValue));
}
```

The method will be decorated with the Function attribute where the stored
procedure name will be specified. The method name will be similar or
equal to the stored procedure name. SQLMetal will infer the method return
type by analyzing the SQL statement that the stored procedure uses. For
this reason there are some situations SQLMetal tool can't handle. If the
stored procedure uses temporary tables or dynamic SQL (by calling the
sp_executesql system-stored procedure), the tool will not be able to infer
the result's type. Therefore, it will not able to define a related method with
a valid return type. These kinds of stored procedures cannot be used with
LINQ to SQL. Finally, the body of the generated method contains a call to
the ExecuteMethodCall method provided by the DataContext class. This
method has two parameters indicating the MethodInfo object for the current
method (useful for discovering the stored procedure name by reflection)
and a collection of parameters that have to be passed to the stored
procedure. Listing 2-20 uses this method to call the related stored
procedure.

*Listing 2-20. Using the Method Associated with a Stored Procedure
to Retrieve the Number of Person Rows in the Database*

```
PeopleDataContext people = new PeopleDataContext();

Console.WriteLine("Person count = {0}",
                  people.uspCountPerson());
```

If we have a stored procedure selecting a set of rows, we can use the same technique to produce a method, calling that stored procedure and returning a collection of objects:

```
create procedure uspGetRoleDescription
    @description varchar(50)
as
    SELECT ID, RoleDescription
    FROM Role
    WHERE RoleDescription LIKE @description
```

The stored procedure in the example returns a set of role rows in which the role description is like a provided parameter. Since the selected columns have been specified in the Role class we can define a method that calls this stored procedure and returns a collection of Role objects.

```
[StoredProcedure(Name = "dbo.uspGetRoleDescription")]
public IEnumerable<Role> uspGetRoleDescription(
  [Parameter(Name = "@description")] string description)
{
  IQueryResults<Role> result =
    ExecuteMethodCall<Role>(this,
      ((MethodInfo)(MethodInfo.GetCurrentMethod())),
                  description);
    return ((IEnumerable<Role>)(result));
}
```

When the stored procedure accepts parameters, we have to decorate each related method parameter with the Parameter attribute where we specify its name. The ExecuteMethodCall<T> method uses the properties contained in the class specified as parameter T to fill the object with the column value returned by the stored procedure. Finally, the IQueryResult<T> interface is converted to IEnumerable<T> in order to be used by the iterator reading its records.

Listing 2-21 shows the code that calls this method.

Listing 2-21. Using the uspGetRoleDescription Method to Retrieve Roles Rows

```
PeopleDataContext people = new PeopleDataContext();

foreach(Role r in people.uspGetRoleDescription("M%"))
{
    Console.WriteLine("Role: {0} {1}", r.ID.ToString(),
        r.RoleDescription);
}
```

The last case supported by LINQ to SQL is for stored procedures using OUTPUT parameters:

```
create procedure uspGetTotalSalaryAmountPerYear
    @year int,
    @amount money output
as
    set @amount = (select sum(SalaryYear)
                    from Salary
                    where year=@year)
    select @amount
```

The stored procedure above computes the total money amount for the salary in a specified year. When the SQLMetal tool encounters this stored procedure it will produce the following method:

```
[Function(Name = "dbo.uspGetTotalSalaryAmountPerYear")]
public ISingleResult<uspGetTotalSalaryAmountPerYearResult>
uspGetTotalSalaryAmountPerYear(
[Parameter(DbType = "Int")] System.Nullable<int> year,
[Parameter(DbType = "Money")]
ref System.Nullable<decimal> amount)
```

```
{
    IExecuteResult result = this.ExecuteMethodCall(this,
        ((MethodInfo)(MethodInfo.GetCurrentMethod())),
                        year,
                        amount);
    amount = ((System.Nullable<decimal>)
            (result.GetParameterValue(1)));

return ((ISingleResult<uspGetTotalSalaryAmountPerYearResult>)
(result.ReturnValue));
}
```

First the OUTPUT parameter is transformed into a ref method parameter.
Then the ISingleResult is used with GetParameterValue() to set the value of
the ref variable. The SQLMetal tool generates a new class to contain the
retrieved records: the uspGetTotalSalaryAmountPerYear class.

Listing 2-22 shows the code necessary to execute this method and retrieve
the total money amount for the year 2004.

*Listing 2-22. Using the Method Related to the Stored Procedure to
Retrieve the Total Money Amount for the Year 2004*

```
PeopleDataContext people = new PeopleDataContext();

decimal? total = 0;
int year = 2004;

people.UspGetTotalSalaryAmountPerYear(year, ref total);

Console.WriteLine(total.ToString());
```

User-Defined Functions

LINQ to SQL also supports *user-defined functions* (UDFs), which return
both scalar values and result sets.

Using the SQLMetal tool's /functions option, we can obtain a new method
in the class that inherits from the DataContext class; the new method is
decorated with attributes for building a SQL statement that calls a UDF.

The following UDF returns the initials of the person whose identifier is specified as an argument:

```
create function udfGetInitials(@id     int)
returns varchar(2)
as
begin
    declare @initials varchar(2)
    set @initials = (SELECT LEFT(FirstName,1) + LEFT(LastName,1)
                     FROM Person
                     WHERE ID = @id)

    return @initials
end
```

Executing the SQLMetal tool to generate entity classes and user-defined function code, we obtain the following method code:

```
[Function(Name = "dbo.udfGetInitials", IsComposable = true)]
public string udfGetInitials([Parameter(DbType = "Int")] Nullable<int> id)
{
    return ((string)(this.ExecuteMethodCall(this,
        ((MethodInfo)(MethodInfo.GetCurrentMethod())),
        id).ReturnValue));
}
```

First the Function attribute is used to decorate the method and inform LINQ that it is associated with the UDF specified with the Name parameter. The IsComposable flag set to true indicates to LINQ to SQL that this is a UDF, not a stored procedure.

Finally, the method's approach is similar to the one seen during stored procedure calling: the ExecuteMethodCall returns an IExecuteResult result. The ReturnValue property is casted to string and returned to the method caller.

Listing 2-23 shows a code snippet in which the UDF is called within a LINQ query to obtain the initials of each person present in the Person table.

Listing 2-23. The UDF Is Transformed into a Method That Can be Called as Usual from Our Code.

```
PeopleDataContext people = new PeopleDataContext();
people.Log = Console.Out;

var query = from p in people.People
            select new {p.ID, Initials = people.UdfGetInitials(p.ID)};

foreach(var row in query)
    Console.WriteLine("PersonID: {0} - Initials: {1}",
                        row.ID, row.Initials);
```

Figure 2-12 shows the output from Listing 2-23.

Figure 2-12. The output shows how the UDF calculates the person's initials.

```
C:\WINDOWS\system32\cmd.exe                                    _ □ ×
SELECT [t0].[ID], [dbo].[udfGetInitials]([t0].[ID]) AS [value]
FROM [Person] AS [t0]

PersonID: 1 - Initials: CO
PersonID: 2 - Initials: TG
PersonID: 3 - Initials: MG
Press any key to continue . . .
```

As Figure 2-12 shows, the SELECT statement built by LINQ contains an inline call to the UDF. That's because we have used the related method within our LINQ query. If we use the method outside a query we will obtain a simple statement like this one:

```
SELECT dbo.udfGetInitials(@p0)
```

Database Creation

Since Microsoft has released a free version of Microsoft SQL Server 2005 called Express Edition, we can easily create an application that stores data using a database instead of XML files or some other data storage. In fact, SQL Server Express Edition can be distributed without limits, allowing us to install and use it even with desktop client applications. Focusing on that feature, a way to create a database on the fly could be really useful.

LINQ to SQL provides a method of the `DataContext` class called `CreateDatabase`. Using the attributes specified in the entity classes, where each column is decorated with options such as column name, column database data type, and so on, LINQ is able to create a new database.

Note   When you need to create a database from scratch using the `CreateDatabase` method you must use the `DbType` option for each column. LINQ uses this information to create the column data type.

Listing in 2-24 shows how you can use `CreateDatabase()` to create a new database.

Listing 2-24. Creating a New Database with the CreateDatabase() Method

```
PeopleDataContext people = new PeopleDataContext(

@"Data Source=.;Initial Catalog=PeopleFromCode;Integrated
        Security=True");

    if (people.DatabaseExists())
        people.DeleteDatabase();

    people.CreateDatabase();
```

Note the connection string that points to a nonexistent database. The `DataContext` class uses the connection string to discover whether the database already exists. Otherwise it uses the catalog option specified in the connection string as database name and creates it. Using the `DatabaseExists` and `DeleteDatabase` methods we can check if the database already exists and if so, drop it.

There are some limitations when using the `CreateDatabase` method to create a database:

- Because stored procedures, UDFs, and triggers are not defined in the entity classes as structure, they are not reproduced.

- Despite the fact that associations could be declared into entity classes, the method is not able to create foreign keys and constraints.

- The application must impersonate a user who has rights to create the database.

LINQ to SQL in Visual Studio 2008

Visual Studio 2008 provides functionality to support LINQ application development. The compiler is upgraded to support LINQ query syntax, and IntelliSense supports almost every LINQ component. Further, a really great tool has been added to Visual Studio: the Linq to SQL Classes Designer. It is similar to SQLMetal in that it produces the code to manage entity classes related to database tables, but it has these advantages:

- It produces entity classes just for specified tables, not for the full database.

- It produces entity class associations using a visual tool.

- It customizes the entity class behavior, letting us choose the stored procedures to run when insert/update/delete commands occur.

- It supports entity class hierarchies.

- It is completely a visual tool and the final result offers a visual representation of classes, associations, and so on within a colored diagram.

A Linq to SQL File Designer Example

Using Linq to SQL File Designer is very easy. Starting from a Windows Application project, you have to add a new `Linq to SQL Classes` item to the solution. Visual Studio then shows you the Linq to SQL Classes Designer together with a new toolbox.

Follow these steps to add database support using Linq to SQL Classes Designer:

1. Launch Visual Studio 2008 and create a new project with File ↗ New Project.

2. Choose the Windows Forms Application template, as shown in Figure 2-13.

Figure 2-13. Creating a new Windows Forms application from Visual Studio 2008

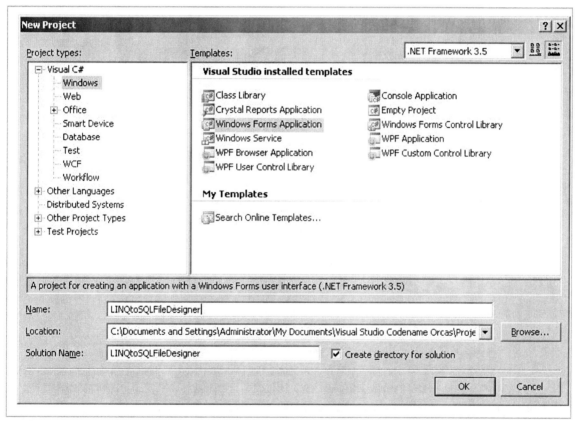

3. From the Solution Explorer, right-click on the solution name and choose Add ↗ New Item from the context menu as shown in Figure 2-14.

Figure 2-14. Adding a new item to the solution

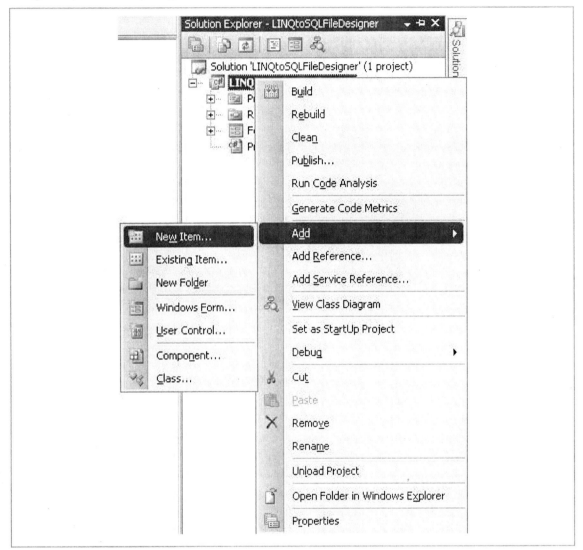

4. From the Add New Item dialog box, select the Linq to SQL Classes template and give it a significant name, as shown in Figure 2-15.

Figure 2-15. Adding a new Linq to SQL File template to the solution

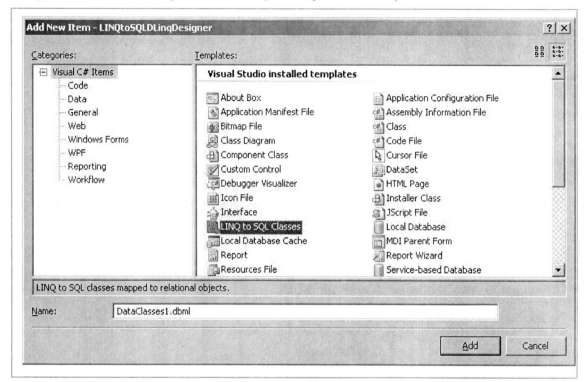

5. At this point Visual Studio will present the Linq to SQL Classes Designer and provide a new toolbox section (see Figure 2-16). You can use the new toolbox to graphically specify the structure of your table.

Figure 2-16. The new Linq to SQL Classes toolbox provided by the Linq to SQL Classes Designer

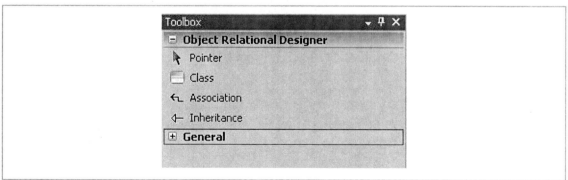

Double-click on the Class item; a new empty entity class is added to the designer, allowing us to start manipulating it. By right-clicking on the entity class we can add new properties or delete them, as shown in Figure 2-17.

Figure 2-17. After adding a new Class we can add new properties or delete the class itself

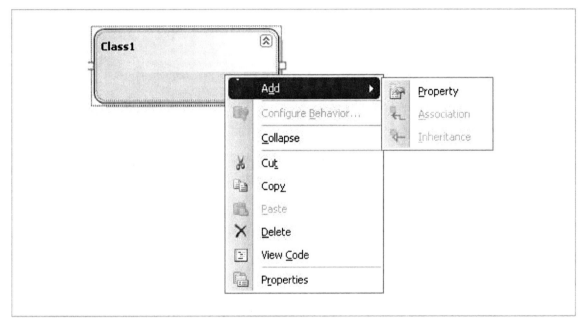

6. Specify properties in the Properties window (see Figure 2-18). You should be accustomed to the property names because they are the same as column attributes.

Figure 2-18. The Properties window shows the Property item properties.

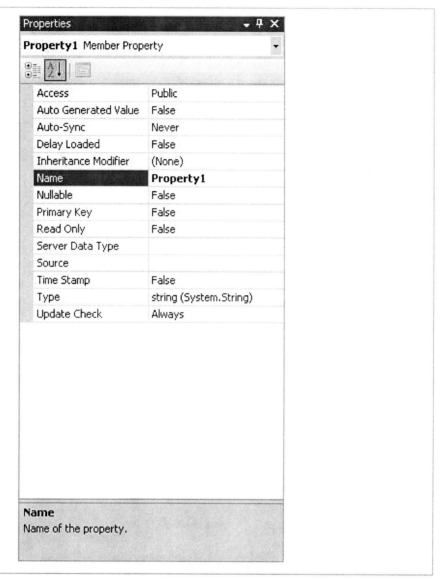

7. Because Linq to SQL Classes Designer supports drag-and-drop from Server Explorer, we are not going to manually create each class from the database. If you can't see Server Explorer, select View ↗ Server Explorer. From Server

Explorer select the Connect to Database button, as shown in Figure 2-19.

Figure 2-19. Connecting to a database from Server Explorer

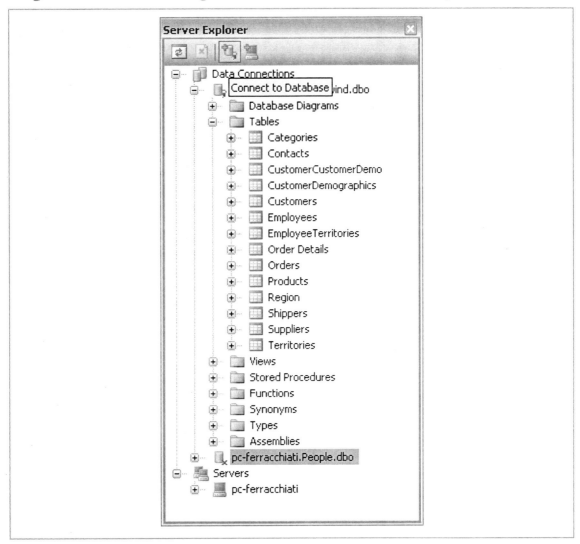

8. From the Add Connection dialog box (shown in Figure 2-20) you specify every parameter—server name, database, and so on—to connect to a

database. Select the database server where the People database has been stored.

Figure 2-20. Add a connection to a database to manage it from the Visual Studio.

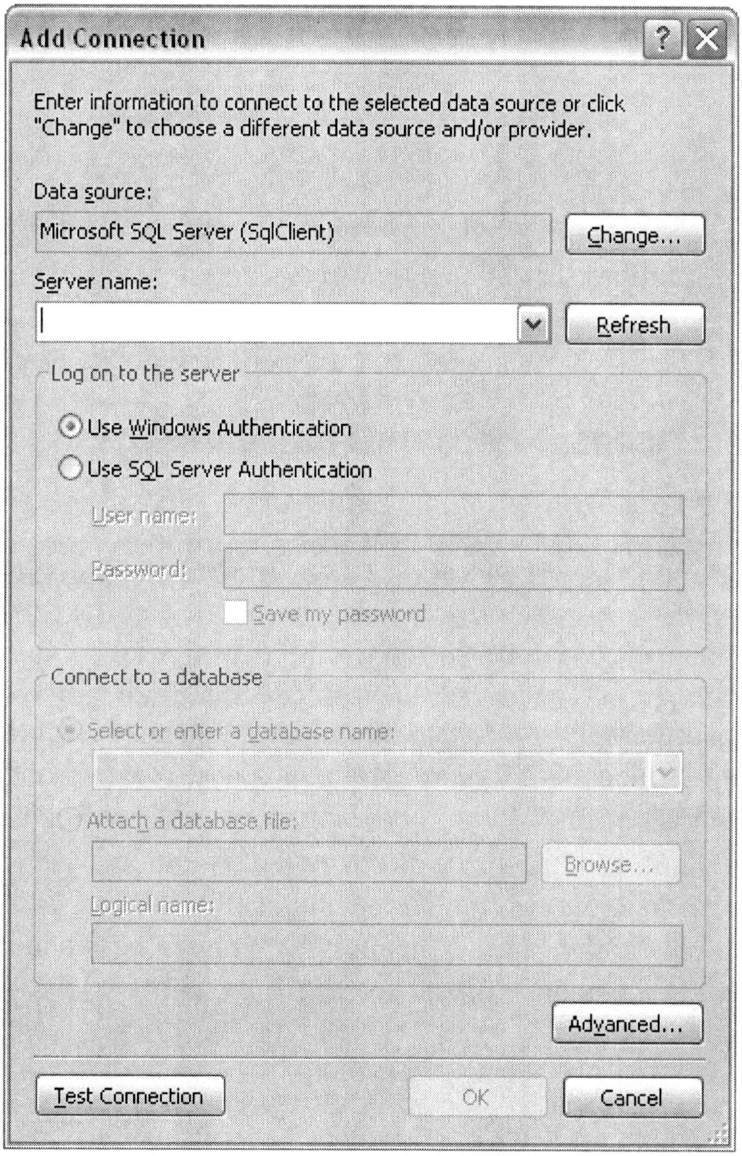

9. Choose a table from Server Explorer and drag it into the Linq to SQL Classes Designer tool. For example, using the People database, drag the **Role** table and drop it into the designer. Visual Studio will present the diagram in Figure 2-21.

Figure 2-21. The Role table is transformed into the Role entity class after dragging and dropping the table from Server Explorer.

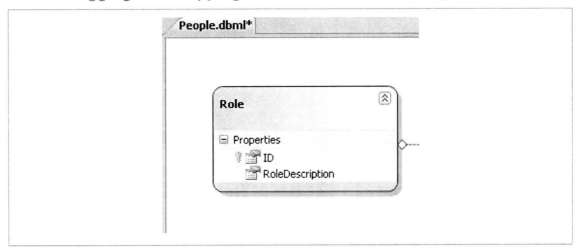

10. This simple operation has generated a diagram with the dragged table and some code (which you can view by selecting the related **,cs** file in Solution Explorer). Now you can drag the **Person** table from Server Explorer and drop it into the Linq to SQL Classes Designer. The final result is shown in Figure 2-22. Because the **Role** and **Person** tables have defined a foreign key relation, the Linq to SQL Classes Designer creates an association between the two entity classes automatically.

Figure 2-22. The association between the Role and Person tables

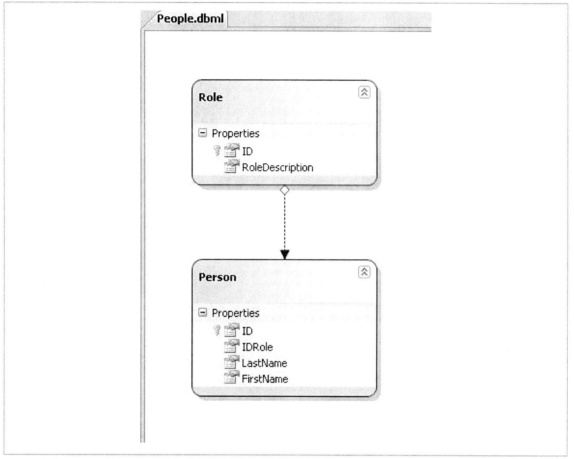

11. We want to show two views containing roles and person rows. When we select a row from the Role view the Person view is refreshed to show related person rows. To accomplish this we can add two **DataGridView** controls to the main form—one called **dgRole** that will contain role rows, and the other called **dgPerson** to contain related person rows.

12. In the **Form1** constructor we have to create an object from the **PeopleDataContext** class generated by the tool to query the database within the source code.

```
private PeopleDataContext db;

public Form1()
{
    InitializeComponent();
    db = new PeopleDataContext();
}
```

13. Now we have to add the Load event handler in the code, and specify the following code:

```
private void Form1_Load(object sender, EventArgs e)
{
    var query = from r in db.Roles
                    select r;

    dgRole.DataSource = query;
    dgPerson.DataSource = dgRole.DataSource;
    dgPerson.DataMember = "Persons";
}
```

The query retrieves all the roles from the database and fills the dgRole data grid. The rest of the code is really interesting because it uses the association between the two entity classes to show only the person-related rows in the data grid. It uses just two simple lines of code!

14. Press CTRL + F5 to build and execute the code. Selecting the role rows shows that the dgPerson grid displays related rows (see Figure 2-23).

Figure 2-23. The Windows form application in execution

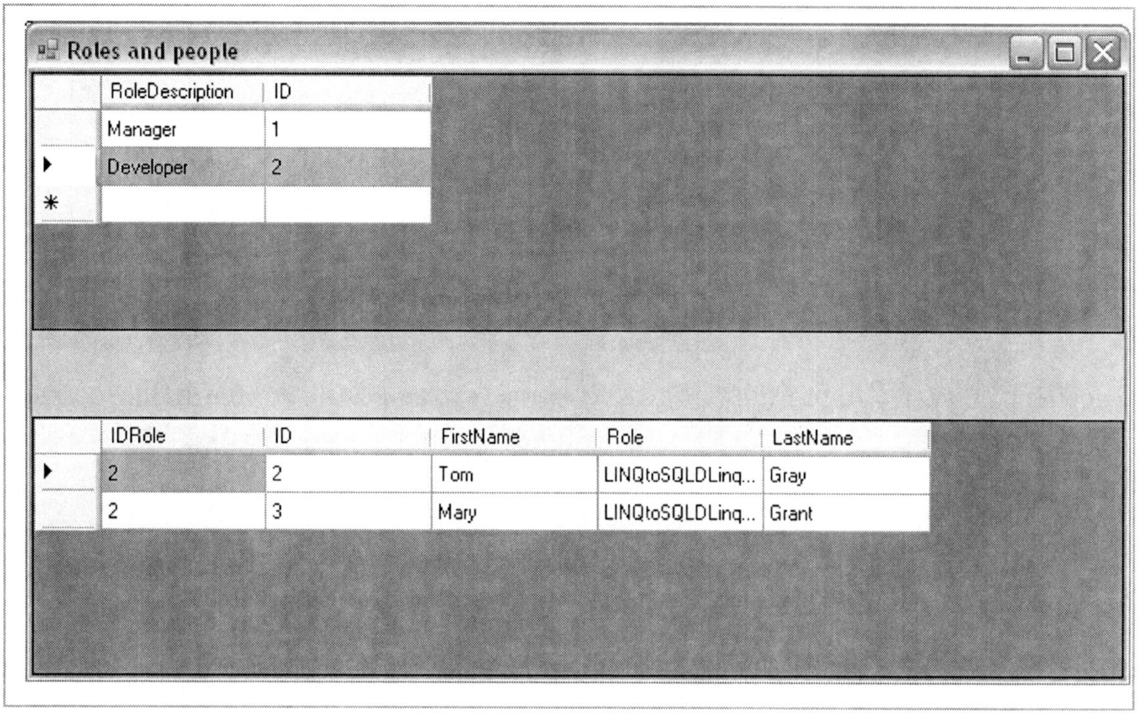

Debugging LINQ Applications

From ScottGu's blog it is possible to download a Visual Studio debugger
add-in: the SQL Server Query Visualizer. Follow this thread to install it
within your Visual Studio 2008:
`http://weblogs.asp.net/scottgu/archive/2007/07/31/linq-to-sql-debug-`
`visualizer.aspx`. This add-in is really useful because it allows us to check
the query syntax built by LINQ before it's sent to the database. Moreover,
it allows us to execute the query from the debugger to discover if the result
is what we expect. We can also modify the query.

To use the visualizer we have to put a breakpoint just before the LINQ
query definition and press the little magnifying-glass icon that appears
when we mouse over the query variable (see Figure 2-24).

Figure 2-24. Pressing the magnifying-glass icon to use the SQL Server Query Visualizer

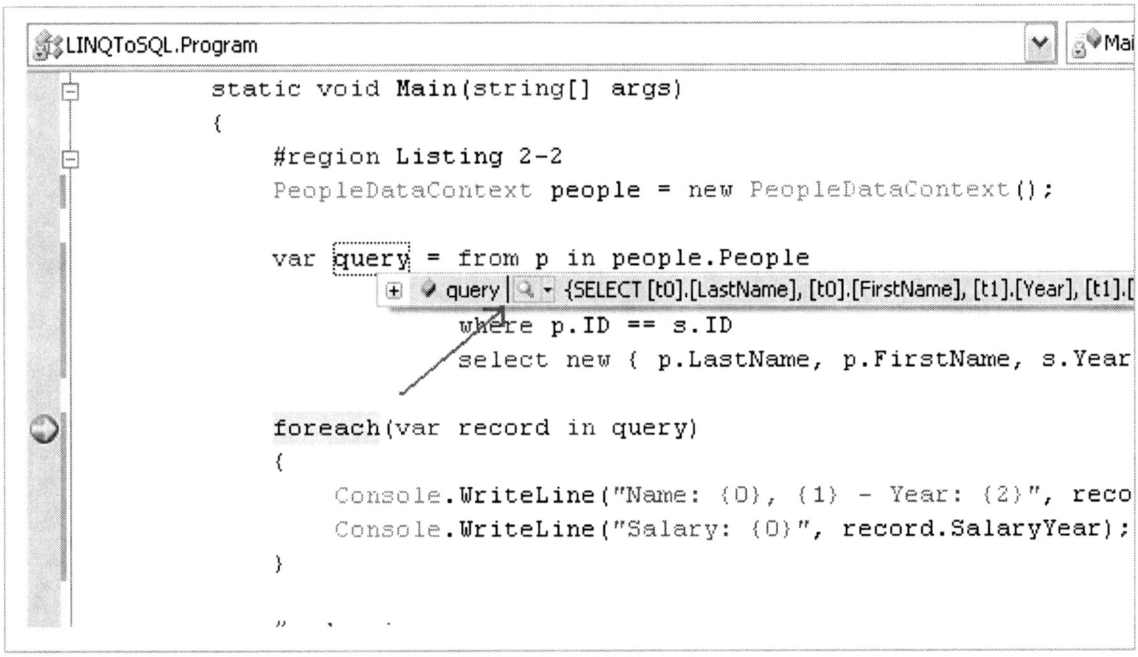

```
LINQToSQL.Program                                                    ✔  🔍Mai

        static void Main(string[] args)
        {
            #region Listing 2-2
            PeopleDataContext people = new PeopleDataContext();

            var query = from p in people.People
                    ⊞  ✔ query  🔍 ▾  {SELECT [t0].[LastName], [t0].[FirstName], [t1].[Year], [t1].[
                          where p.ID == s.ID
                          select new { p.LastName, p.FirstName, s.Year

            foreach(var record in query)
            {
                Console.WriteLine("Name: {0}, {1} - Year: {2}", reco
                Console.WriteLine("Salary: {0}", record.SalaryYear);
            }

            "   '    '
```

After pressing the magnifying-glass icon the Query Visualizer tool will appear within the debugger (see Figure 2-25).

Figure 2-25. The SQL Server Query Visualizer in action

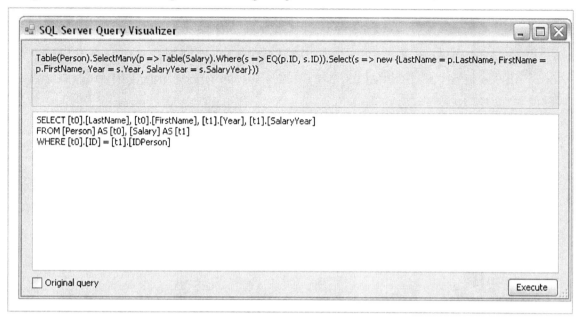

The window is divided in two sections; the upper section is a read-only text area where the LINQ query is displayed after the compiler has transformed it using lambda expressions and methods. The lower section is a writable text area containing the SQL to be executed against the database. The SQL can be executed by clicking the Execute button (see Figure 2-26).

Figure 2-26. Pressing the Execute button provided by the SQL Server Query Visualizer executes the query, showing the result in the QueryResult window while the application is waiting on a breakpoint.

LastName	FirstName	Year	SalaryYear
Optimistic	Concurrency	2004	10000.0000
Optimistic	Concurrency	2005	15000.0000

Placing the breakpoint just after the query variable definition illustrates that LINQ to SQL uses deferred query execution. Remember that query execution starts only after the query is iterated through a `foreach` statement or when a caching method such as `ToList()` is used. The debugger allows us to discover an additional aspect during query execution. Consider the code snippet in Listing 2-25.

Listing 2-25. Iterating Through Role and Person Rows

```
PeopleDataContext people = new PeopleDataContext();
people.Log = Console.Out;

var query = from r in people.Roles
            select r;

foreach (var role in query)
{
    foreach(var person in role.People)
    {
        Console.WriteLine("Person: {0} {1}", person.FirstName,
            person.LastName);
    }
}
```

The code uses the association declared in `Role` and `Person` entity classes to iterate through role rows and, with an inner `foreach` statement, to print the persons that have each role.

If you put a breakpoint on the query variable within the `foreach` statement and press F5 to start the debugger, you'll see that no query has been sent to the database. Press F10 to go a step further; the first query will be printed in the console application (see Figure 2-27).

Figure 2-27. The first query is sent to the database just after the query variable is iterated.

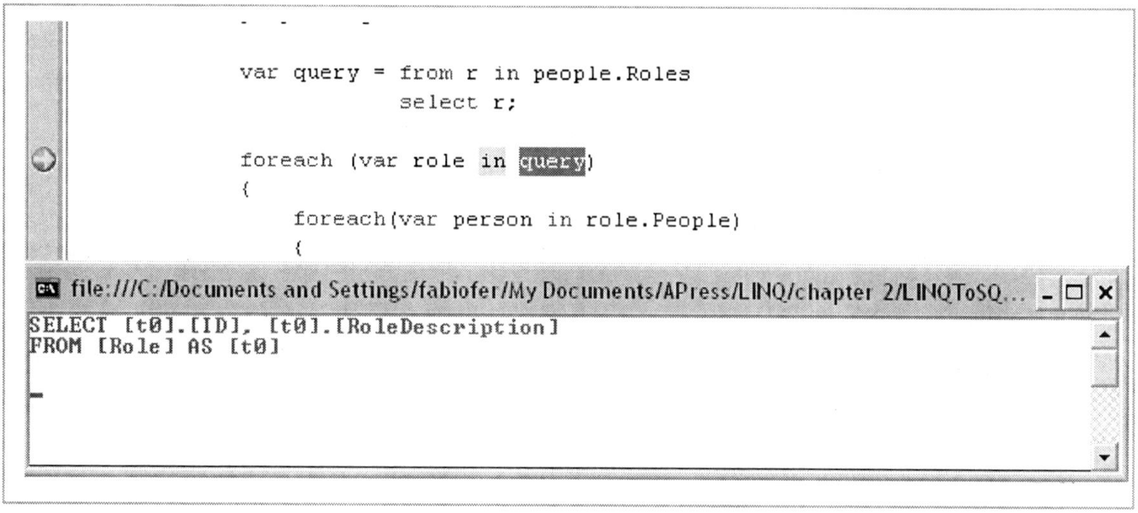

```
            var query = from r in people.Roles
                        select r;

            foreach (var role in query)
            {
                foreach(var person in role.People)
                {
```

```
file:///C:/Documents and Settings/fabiofer/My Documents/APress/LINQ/chapter 2/LINQToSQ...  _ □ ×
SELECT [t0].[ID], [t0].[RoleDescription]
FROM [Role] AS [t0]
```

Continue pressing F10 to see that a SELECT statement is sent to the database to select person rows each time a new role is processed (see Figure 2-28).

Figure 2-28. Each time a new role row is processed a new SELECT statement is sent to the database to retrieve related person rows.

```
var query = from r in people.Roles
            select r;

foreach (var role in query)
{
    foreach(var person in role.People)
    {
```

```
file:///C:/Documents and Settings/fabiofer/My Documents/APress/LINQ/chapter 2/LINQToSQ...

SELECT [t0].[ID], [t0].[RoleDescription]
FROM [Role] AS [t0]

SELECT [t0].[FirstName], [t0].[LastName], [t0].[IDRole], [t0].[ID]
FROM [Person] AS [t0]
WHERE [t0].[IDRole] = @p0

Person: Carl Lewis
Person: Fabio Ferracchiati
SELECT [t0].[FirstName], [t0].[LastName], [t0].[IDRole], [t0].[ID]
FROM [Person] AS [t0]
WHERE [t0].[IDRole] = @p0
```

As you can imagine, when you process many rows the database is queried too many times and performance is far from optimal. In such cases, to avoid the deferred loading of rows you can use the LoadWith method provided by the DataLoadOptions class, as shown in Listing 2-26.

Listing 2-26. Using LoadWith<T>() to Preload the person Rows, Thereby Avoiding the Deferred Loading of Rows

```
PeopleDataContext people = new PeopleDataContext();
people.Log = Console.Out;

DataLoadOptions shape = new DataLoadOptions();
shape.LoadWith<Role>(r => r.People);
```

```
people.LoadOptions = shape;

var query = from r in people.Roles
            select r;

foreach (var role in query)
{
    foreach (var person in role.People)
    {
        Console.WriteLine("Person: {0} {1}",
                          person.FirstName,
                          person.LastName);
    }
}
```

If you execute the debugger after setting a breakpoint on the query variable you'll see that just two queries are sent to the database: one to retrieve all the roles and one to retrieve all the people (see Figure 2-29).

Figure 2-29. When using LoadWith<T>() just two SELECT statements are sent to the database.

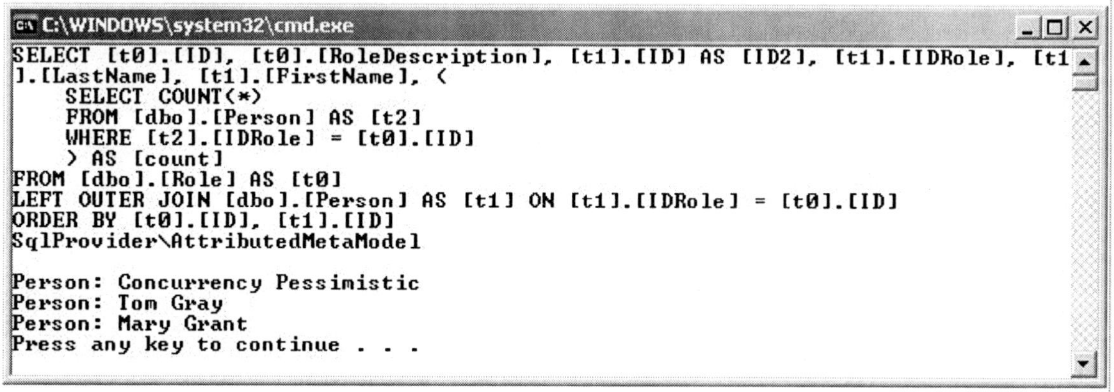

The DataLoadOptions class provides a new method called AssociateWith<>, which is useful to define a subquery against the prefetched records.

LINQ to DataSet

In the previous section, you saw how LINQ to SQL supports ADO.NET transactions. This is not the only integration between the "old" ADO.NET library and the "new" LINQ to SQL. In fact, LINQ to SQL can use ADO.NET DataSets with LINQ to DataSet.

With some limitations, LINQ to DataSet allows developers to use DataSets as normal data sources using the usual LINQ query syntax.

Listing 2-27 shows a simple example that uses a LINQ query to fill a typed dataset.

Listing 2-27. Filling a Typed DataTable with the CopyToDataTable Method

```
dsPeople ds = new dsPeople();
dsPeople.RoleRow row = ds.Role.NewRoleRow();
row.ID = 1;
row.RoleDescription = "Manager";
ds.Role.AddRoleRow(row);

row = ds.Role.NewRoleRow();
row.ID = 2;
row.RoleDescription = "Developer";
ds.Role.AddRoleRow(row);

var q = from role in ds.Role
        select role;

dsPeople.RoleDataTable t = new dsPeople.RoleDataTable();
q.CopyToDataTable(t, LoadOption.OverwriteChanges);
```

dsPeople is a typed DataSet added to the Visual Studio project. When you use Visual Studio to create your DataSet objects you can use the DataSet Designer tool, which makes it possible to drag and drop tables from Server Explorer (the same way as when using Linq to SQL Classes Designer). In the dsPeople data set I added the Role table. This operation has automatically created a typed `DataSet` that contains the `Role` table together with some other methods and objects.

The prefilled `DataSet` object is used in the LINQ query to retrieve all its records. Then the `CopyToDataTable` method, provided as an extension of the `IEnumerable<T>` interface, is used to fill a typed `DataTable` object. This last object will be used in the next code snippet to perform another LINQ query to filter the records.

The `CopyToDataTable` method has been added to load a `DataTable` from a Linq to DataSet query. It provides two versions: the former returns a new `DataTable` and doesn't accept parameters while the latter fills an existing `DataTable` provided as parameter, plus a second parameter indicating the `LoadOption` options (that is, overwrite records).

Note   In existing ADO.NET applications `DataSet` objects are filled with `DataAdapter` objects or with other techniques. LINQ to DataSet is completely indifferent about how you fill a `DataSet`.

In Listing 2-28 we use the filled `dsPeople` `DataSet` just like any data source, and a LINQ query to retrieve a role.

Listing 2-28. A Typed DataSet Is Queryable Just Like Any Other Data Source.

```
var query = from r in t
            where r.ID == 1
            select r;

foreach(var row in query)
{
    Console.WriteLine("Role: {0} {1}", row.ID, row.RoleDescription);
}
```

The `Role` property contained in the `ds` `DataSet` is iterated by using the `Rows` collection to look for the row whose identifier is equal to 1.

LINQ to DataSet adds support for untyped `DataSet`s as well. In this case the code is a bit more complex to write because LINQ has to acquire more information from the query. Listing 2-29 shows how an untyped data set can be filled using a LINQ query.

Listing 2-29. Filling an Untyped Data Table Using a LINQ Query and the CopyToDataTable Method

```
dsPeople ds = new dsPeople();
dsPeople.RoleRow row = ds.Role.NewRoleRow();
row.ID = 1;
row.RoleDescription = "Manager";
ds.Role.AddRoleRow(row);

row = ds.Role.NewRoleRow();
row.ID = 2;
row.RoleDescription = "Developer";
ds.Role.AddRoleRow(row);

var q = from role in ds.Role
        select role;

DataTable dtRole = q.CopyToDataTable();
```

The `CopyToDataTable` extended method iterates through the results of the query, creating a new `DataTable` object filled with `DataColumn` objects and values.

Querying an untyped data set is a bit more complex because we have to use the `Field<T>` class to specify the column's data type; see Listing 2-30.

```
var query = from p in dtRole.AsEnumerable()
              where p.Field<string>("RoleDescription") == "Manager"
              select p;

foreach (var record in query)
{
    Console.WriteLine("Role: {0} {1}",
      record.Field<int>("ID"),
      record.Field<string>("RoleDescription"));
}
```

First of all, the `DataTable` class doesn't provide an implementation of the `IEnumerable` and `IQueryable` interfaces, so the `dtPerson` object cannot be used in the LINQ query directly. We have to use the `AsEnumerable` extended method, which generates an `IEnumerable<T>` composed of `DataTable` rows.

Second, we need to use the `Field<T>` generic method to specify the data type of the `DataTable` column we are going to manage. This is necessary because when using the classic syntax to access a `DataTable` row (e.g. `p["LastName"]`) we should cast the return type and also use the `IsNull` method of the `DataRow` class to check if the data is null. The `Field<T>` generic method does all this automatically, plus checks null values when the column accepts nulls (e.g., using `Field<string?>`).

As stated previously, LINQ to DataSet has some limitations that should be removed eventually. For example, the `CopyToDataTable` method doesn't understand relationships and cannot produce multiple data tables. Moreover, there is no way to use LINQ to DataSet to update database rows after they are retrieved by a LINQ query into a data set object.

Summary

In this chapter you saw how to create entity classes and how, thanks to new attributes and their properties, you can easily map those classes to database tables. Then you analyzed `DataContext` functionality for interfacing with databases. You also saw how defining associations between entity classes simulates relationships between tables.

You then looked at advanced features, such as optimistic concurrency, stored procedures, and user-defined functions.

Finally, you used the Visual Studio Linq to SQL Classes Designer tool to create entity classes, and you used its improved debugger. The chapter concluded by analyzing LINQ integration with ADO.NET, specifically with `DataSets`.

In the next chapter we'll use LINQ to manage XML data.

Chapter 3: LINQ to XML

In this chapter we'll analyze LINQ to XML in detail. We'll start by viewing XML documents as data sources and then we'll use LINQ queries to retrieve XML data. Then we'll look at how to use LINQ to XML to produce XML documents.

Introduction

Language Integrated Query lets you focus on what you have to do and not on how to do it. With this in mind, XML becomes just another data source for LINQ.

From a developer perspective, XML is not an easy thing to manage because the World Wide Web Consortium's document object model (DOM) is not a simple library to use. The DOM framework often requires you to write a lot of code to produce even a little XML output. Moreover, if you need to search for a particular item within an XML document you have to use DOM features, such as XPath, based on query syntax that is not intuitive. XPath uses a searching model that is not similar to other query languages, such as SQL, and you have to spend time to learn it.

Eliminating such complexity is the main motive behind LINQ to XML. .NET offers its own library to manage XML, but LINQ to XML goes a big step further; it integrates the LINQ standard query operators with XML documents. In addition, LINQ to XML offers classes for easily creating XML.

Querying XML

Since LINQ to XML supports the LINQ standard query operators, an XML document can be loaded in memory and then queried with the usual LINQ query syntax.

Let's start by analyzing a simple query using a couple of important LINQ to XML classes. Listing 3-1 is the XML representation of our People database.

Listing 3-1. The XML Representation of the People Database

```xml
<?xml version="1.0" encoding="utf-8" ?>
<people>
    <!--Person section-->
    <person>
        <id>1</id>
        <firstname>Carl</firstname>
        <lastname>Lewis</lastname>
        <idrole>1</idrole>
    </person>
    <person>
        <id>2</id>
        <firstname>Tom</firstname>
        <lastname>Gray</lastname>
        <idrole>2</idrole>
    </person>
    <person>
        <id>3</id>
        <firstname>Mary</firstname>
        <lastname>Grant</lastname>
        <idrole>2</idrole>
    </person>
    <person>
        <id>4</id>
        <firstname>Fabio Claudio</firstname>
        <lastname>Ferracchiati</lastname>
        <idrole>1</idrole>
    </person>
    <!--Role section-->
    <role>
        <id>1</id>
        <roledescription>Manager</roledescription>
    </role>
    <role>
        <id>2</id>
        <roledescription>Developer</roledescription>
    </role>
```

```
    <!--Salary section-->
    <salary>
        <idperson id="1" year="2004" salaryyear="10000,0000" />
        <idperson id="1" year="2005" salaryyear="15000,0000" />
    </salary>
</people>
```

In Listing 3-1 the XDocument class provides the Elements method that returns items from the XElement class. The XElement class represents the core of the entire LINQ to XML library. An XElement object is the representation of an element within an XML document. Each node, as well as each leaf, in the XML document is an element. As you can see from the code in Listing 3-2, to obtain an element's value you have to use the Elements method repeatedly. When observing the XML structure you can see that the people element is the root and the person element appears four times to represent four rows in the people data source. Using the Elements method provided by the XElement class you can retrieve a collection of elements and iterate through them. So, by appending the Elements("person") method call to the Elements("people") method call you can retrieve all four person elements in the XML document.

The where condition filters the person elements to retrieve the one whose identifier is equal to one.

Listing 3-2. Retrieving a Person's Record from an XML Document

```
XDocument xml = XDocument.Load(@"..\..\People.xml");

var query = from p in xml.Elements("people").Elements("person")
            where (int)p.Element("id") == 1
            select p;

foreach(var record in query)
{
    Console.WriteLine("Person: {0} {1}",
        record.Element("firstname").Value,
        record.Element("lastname").Value);
}
```

Finally, the **foreach** statement iterates through the elements and prints the
name of each person. You use the **Value** property to retrieve an element's
value.

The **XDocument** class is very similar to the **XElement** class (it contains the
same methods, properties, etc.) but it represents the root element of an
XML document. In our example, the **XDocument** object represents the **people**
element. Its **Load** method will load the XML document into memory,
allowing us to use the **XDocument** object for queries.

If you don't care about the root element and just want to go straight to a
particular element, you can use the **Load** method of the **XElement** class. In
Listing 3-3 you can see the same query applied to our XML data source but
using less code.

Listing 3-3. Retrieving Person Data by Using Less Code

```
XElement xml = XElement.Load(@"..\..\People.xml");

var query = from p in xml.Elements("person")
            where (int)p.Element("id") == 1
            select p;

foreach(var record in query)
{
    Console.WriteLine("Person: {0} {1}",
                                record.Element("firstname"),
                                record.Element("lastname"));
}
```

You can search directly for person records without calling the **Elements**
method for the root element. Moreover, if you omit the **Value** property

(used in Listing 3-2), you can call the ToString method, which returns the full element with its start and end tags (see Figure 3-1).

Figure 3-1. Omitting the Value property, the output will be the full element.

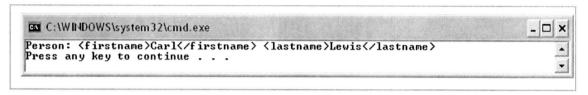

```
C:\WINDOWS\system32\cmd.exe
Person: <firstname>Carl</firstname> <lastname>Lewis</lastname>
Press any key to continue . . .
```

Note   Casting an Element to a string is equivalent to using its Value property.

Searching for Attribute Values

The following code shows salary information stored in idperson attributes:

```
<salary>
    <idperson year="2004" salaryyear="10000,0000">1</idperson>
    <idperson year="2005" salaryyear="15000,0000">1</idperson>
</salary>
```

Obviously, LINQ to XML provides a way to query elements by their attributes. (See Listing 3-4.)

Listing 3-4. Querying by Attribute Values

```
XElement xml = XElement.Load(@"..\..\People.xml");

var query = from s in xml.Elements("salary").Elements("idperson")
            where (int)s.Attribute("year") == 2004
            select s;

foreach(var record in query)
{
    Console.WriteLine("Amount: {0}", (string)
```

```
                    record.Attribute("salaryyear"));
    }
```

The **XAttribute** class represents the attributes of an element within an XML document. The **Attribute** method returns the value of the attribute whose name is specified as its argument.

The Descendants and Ancestors Methods

When elements are deeply nested, you can use the **Descendants** method to quickly navigate to the desired element. Listing 3-5 shows how to navigate down into nested elements using this quicker way.

Listing 3-5. Using the Descendants Method to Navigate Down an XML Tree

```
XElement xml = XElement.Load(@"..\..\People.xml");

var query = from p in xml.Descendants("person")
            join s in xml.Descendants("idperson")
            on (int)p.Element("id") equals (int)s.Attribute("id")
            select new {FirstName=p.Element("firstname").Value,
                        LastName=p.Element("lastname").Value,
                        Amount=s.Attribute("salaryyear").Value};

foreach(var record in query)
{
    Console.WriteLine("Person: {0} {1}, Salary {2}",record.FirstName,
                                                     record.LastName,
                                                     record.Amount);
}
```

The code in Listing 3-5 joins two sections within the XML data source: **person** and **salary**. As you can see, the query syntax is the same as that used for in-memory objects and database tables and views.

Conversely, the **Ancestors** method goes up through an XML tree until it reaches the root element. In Listing 3-6, both methods are used to navigate the XML document.

```
XElement xml = XElement.Load(@"..\..\People.xml");

var record = xml.Descendants("firstname").First();
foreach(var tag in record.Ancestors())
    Console.WriteLine(tag.Name);
```

First the `Descendants` method returns a collection of `firstname` elements; however, if we use the `First` standard operator, just the first element will be retrieved. The cursor in the XML tree now points to the first `firstname` element, containing the `Carl` value, so if we use the `Ancestors` method to rise to the top of the document, the collection of the `XElement` items will contain two tags: `person` and `people`.

Note   The `Descendants` and `Ancestors` methods do not include the current node. For example, if you start from the root node you'll retrieve all the elements except the root. You can use the `SelfAndDescendants` and `SelfAndAncestors` methods to include the current node.

Querying XML for Content Type

We can use LINQ to XML to query not only for values, but also for types. For instance, our sample XML data source contains three comments. We can search for all the comments as in Listing 3-7.

Listing 3-7. Retrieving All the Comments in an XML Document

```
XElement xml = XElement.Load(@"..\..\People.xml");

IEnumerable<XComment> record = xml.Nodes().OfType<XComment>();
foreach(XComment comment in record)
    Console.WriteLine(comment);
```

The XComment class represents XML comments. Note that we used the Nodes method instead of the Elements method. Examine Figure 3-2 carefully to better understand the hierarchy between LINQ to XML classes.

Figure 3-2. The LINQ to XML class hierarchy

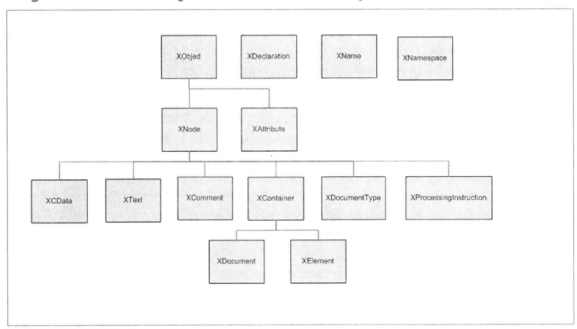

The XElement class is not directly linked to the XComment class, so if we want to retrieve comments we have to use the XNode class. For this reason,, by using the Nodes method of XElement we can obtain a collection of Node objects. Using the OfType standard operator we can filter the objects for the specified type—in Listing 3-7, XComment.

Querying an XML Document That Uses Schemas

XML elements are often associated with specific namespaces, and their names are prefixed with a namespace identifier For example, Microsoft Office 2003 adds XML support for applications such as Microsoft Word, Microsoft Excel, and so on. If you save a simple Word file in XML format, you get an XML document similar to the snippet in Listing 3-8.

Listing 3-8. A Microsoft Word Document Saved Using the XML Format

```
<?xml version="1.0" encoding="UTF-8" standalone="yes"?>
<?mso-application progid="Word.Document"?>
<w:wordDocument
xmlns:w="http://schemas.microsoft.com/office/word/2003/wordml"
xmlns:v="urn:schemas-microsoft-com:vml"
xmlns:w10="urn:schemas-microsoft-com:office:word"

xmlns:sl="http://schemas.microsoft.com/schemaLibrary/2003/core"
xmlns:aml="http://schemas.microsoft.com/aml/2001/core"

xmlns:wx="http://schemas.microsoft.com/office/word/2003/auxHint"
xmlns:o="urn:schemas-microsoft-com:office:office"
xmlns:dt="uuid:C2F41010-65B3-11d1-A29F-00AA00C14882"

xmlns:wsp="http://schemas.microsoft.com/office/word/2003/wordml/sp2"
w:macrosPresent="no"
w:embeddedObjPresent="no"
w:ocxPresent="no"
xml:space="preserve">
<w:ignoreElements
w:val="http://schemas.microsoft.com/office/word/2003/wordml/sp2"/>
<o:DocumentProperties>
    <o:Title>Hello LINQ to XML</o:Title>
    <o:Author>Fabio Claudio Ferracchiati</o:Author>
    <o:LastAuthor>Fabio Claudio Ferracchiati</o:LastAuthor>
    <o:Revision>1</o:Revision>
    <o:TotalTime>1</o:TotalTime>
    <o:Created>2006-08-20T07:54:00Z</o:Created>
    <o:LastSaved>2006-08-20T07:55:00Z</o:LastSaved>
    <o:Pages>1</o:Pages>
    <o:Words>1</o:Words>
    <o:Characters>12</o:Characters>
    <o:Company>APress</o:Company>
    <o:Lines>1</o:Lines>
    <o:Paragraphs>1</o:Paragraphs>
    <o:CharactersWithSpaces>12</o:CharactersWithSpaces>
    <o:Version>11.8026</o:Version>
</o:DocumentProperties>
<w:fonts>
    <w:defaultFonts w:ascii="Times New Roman"
```

```
            w:fareast="Times New Roman"
            w:h-ansi="Times New Roman"
            w:cs="Times New Roman"/>
</w:fonts>
...
...

</w:wordDocument>
```

To query for the Word file's author, we have to search for the <o:Author> tag. The o: prefix identifies the XML namespace defined as

```
xmlns:o="urn:schemas-microsoft-com:office:office"
```

We have to add this information to our LINQ to XML code as shown in Listing 3-9.

Listing 3-9. Querying an XML Document That Uses Namespaces

```
        XElement xml = XElement.Load(@"..\..\Hello_LINQ to XML.xml");
        XNamespace o = "urn:schemas-microsoft-com:office:office";

        var query = from w in xml.Descendants(o + "Author")
                        select w;
        foreach (var record in query)
            Console.WriteLine("Author: {0}", (string)record);
```

The XNamespace class represents and XML namespace. If we concatenate the o object with "Author", the Descendants method will go through the XML document until it reaches the Author tag for the namespace represented by the o object.

You can search for a particular attribute in a similar way. In Listing 3-10 the code searches for the default font style used in the Word document.

Listing 3-10. Retrieving the Attribute's Value Prefixed with the Namespace Shortcut

```
        XElement xml = XElement.Load(@"..\..\Hello_LINQ to XML.xml");
        XNamespace w = "http://schemas.microsoft.com/office/word/2003/wordml";

        XElement defaultFonts = xml.Descendants(w + "defaultFonts").First();
```

```
Console.WriteLine("Default Fonts: {0}",
    (string)defaultFonts.Attribute(w + "ascii"));
```

After the `Descendants` method reached the first `w:DefaultFonts` element, we used the `XElement` object's `Attribute` method to retrieve the `w:ascii` attribute. Note that the namespace must be concatenated to the attribute name in the same way as for the parent element.

The ElementsBeforeSelf and ElementsAfterSelf Methods

It's often necessary to retrieve child elements starting from the current node. This is easy to do by using the `ElementsBeforeSelf` and `ElementsAfterSelf` methods, which retrieve a collection of sibling `XElement` items that occur before the current element and after the current element, respectively. Listing 3-11 shows both methods in action.

Listing 3-11. Using the ElementsBeforeSelf and ElementsAfterSelf Methods

```
XElement xml = XElement.Load(@"..\..\People.xml");

XElement firstName = xml.Descendants("firstname").First();

Console.WriteLine("Before <firstname>");
foreach(var tag in firstName.ElementsBeforeSelf())
    Console.WriteLine(tag.Name);

Console.WriteLine("");
Console.WriteLine("After <firstname>");
foreach(var tag in firstName.ElementsAfterSelf())
    Console.WriteLine(tag.Name);
```

After we've positioned the cursor over the first `firstname` element, calling the two methods will produce the output shown in Figure 3-3.

Figure 3-3. The output shows the XML tags before and after the current XML tag.

Note   If you want to retrieve other XML information, such as comments, you have to use the Node versions of ElementsBeforeSelf and ElementsAfterSelf, NodesBeforeSelf, and NodesAfterSelf.

Miscellaneous Functionalities

The XElement class provides other useful properties to easily obtain access to XML-document information. In this section we will look at them individually.

Parent

This property allows us to retrieve the parent element of the current node, as Listing 3-12 shows.

Listing 3-12. Using the Parent Property to Retrieve the Parent Node of the firstname Element

```csharp
XElement xml = XElement.Load(@"..\..\People.xml");

XElement firstName = xml.Descendants("firstname").First();

Console.WriteLine(firstName.Parent);
```

The parent node of `firstname` is `person`, so the output of this code snippet will be the full `person` element (see Figure 3-4).

Figure 3-4. The output of the code snippet in Listing 3-12

```
C:\WINDOWS\system32\cmd.exe                                    - □ ×
<person>
  <id>1</id>
  <firstname>Carl</firstname>
  <lastname>Lewis</lastname>
  <idrole>1</idrole>
</person>
Press any key to continue . . .
```

HasElements and HasAttributes

These properties check if the current element has child elements or attributes. (See Listing 3-13.)

Listing 3-13. Using HasElements and HasAttributes to Check if the Current Node Has Child Elements and Attributes, Respectively

```
XElement xml = XElement.Load(@"..\..\People.xml");

XElement firstName = xml.Descendants("firstname").First();

Console.WriteLine("FirstName tag has attributes: {0}",
    firstName.HasAttributes);
Console.WriteLine("FirstName tag has child elements: {0}",
    firstName.HasElements);
Console.WriteLine("FirstName tag's parent has attributes: {0}",
firstName.Parent.HasAttributes);
Console.WriteLine("FirstName tag's parent has child elements: {0}",
firstName.Parent.HasElements);
```

After the cursor reaches the first `firstname` element by using the `Descendants` method, the `HasAttributes` and `HasElements` properties check if both the `firstname` element and its parent have attributes and child elements. Figure 3-5 shows the output of this code snippet.

Figure 3-5. The HasElements and HasAttributes properties in action

```
C:\WINDOWS\system32\cmd.exe                                   _ □ ×
FirstName tag has attributes: False
FirstName tag has child elements: False
FirstName tag's parent has attributes: False
FirstName tag's parent has child elements: True
Press any key to continue . . . _
```

IsEmpty

This property checks if the current element contains a value or whether it is empty. (See Listing 3-14.)

Listing 3-14. Using the IsEmpty Property to Check if Some Elements Are Empty

```
        XElement xml = XElement.Load(@"..\..\People.xml");

        XElement firstName = xml.Descendants("firstname").First();

Console.WriteLine("Is FirstName tag empty? {0}", firstName.IsEmpty ?
            "Yes" : "No");

XElement idPerson = xml.Descendants("idperson").First();

Console.WriteLine("Is idperson tag empty? {0}",
                idPerson.IsEmpty ? "Yes" : "No");
```

Figure 3-6 shows the output of this code snippet. If you look at the XML data source (Listing 3-1) you'll see that the firstname element is not empty because it contains the Carl value. You'll also see that the idperson tag is empty (and has only attributes).

Figure 3-6. The output of the code snippet using IsEmpty

Declaration

Using this property we can retrieve information about the XML document declaration. In Listing 3-15 we load the XML document using the XDocument class because it fills the LINQ to XML classes with all the possible information, such as the XML declaration, namespaces, and so on.

In Listing 3-15 we use the Declaration property to retrieve Encoding, Version, and Standalone information from the XML document declaration.

Listing 3-15. Using the Declaration Property

```
XDocument xml = XDocument.Load(@"..\..\Hello_LINQ to XML.xml");

Console.WriteLine("Encoding: {0}", xml.Declaration.Encoding);
Console.WriteLine("Version: {0}", xml.Declaration.Version);
Console.WriteLine("Standalone: {0}", xml.Declaration.Standalone);
```

Figure 3-7 shows the output of Listing 3-15.

Figure 3-7. The output of the code snippet using the Declaration property

Creating and Modifying XML Documents

LINQ to XML doesn't only provide for queries; it also provides for creating and modifying XML documents. Thanks to a feature called *functional construction*, you can create XML documents in an easier way than with the W3C DOM library.

We'll use functional construction to create an XML document from scratch, and then use other LINQ to XML features to manage it.

Finally, we'll look at a couple of examples that integrate LINQ to XML with LINQ to SQL to generate XML output from a database query.

Creating an XML Document from Scratch

If you are accustomed to using the W3C DOM library or the .NET Framework implementation of it, you'll find LINQ to XML very easy and more intuitive to use. The very simple code snippet that follows creates a new person element, followed by its elements:

```
XElement xml = new XElement("people",
                new XElement("person",
                    new XElement("id", 1),
                    new XElement("firstname", "Carl"),
                    new XElement("lastname", "Lewis"),
                    new XElement("idrole", 2)));
```

The functional construction model allows us to use the LINQ to XML classes in a "linked" way. You can create objects with a hierarchical structure that it is similar to the one used in an XML document. Moreover, it is a top-down approach to XML document creation that is more intuitive than the bottom-up approach of the W3C libraries. So the first element to create is the root, people:

```
XElement xml = new XElement("people",
```

To its constructor we can pass another XElement object (person) that will become the child element of people:

```
XElement xml = new XElement("people",
                new XElement("person",
```

We pass other XElement objects to the person constructor to define its children:

```
new XElement("person",
    new XElement("id", 1),
    new XElement("firstname", "Carl"),
    new XElement("lastname", "Lewis"),
    new XElement("idrole", 2)));
```

The XML document will look like this:

```
<people>
  <person>
    <id>1</id>
    <firstname>Carl</firstname>
    <lastname>Lewis</lastname>
    <idrole>2</idrole>
  </person>
</people>
```

Functional construction is based on the XElement class's constructor, which accepts an array of param objects:

```
public XElement(XName name, params object[] contents)
```

Because this constructor accepts an array of generic object types, we can pass it any kind of information, such as the following:

- An XElement object that will be added as child element

- An XAttribute object that will be used as an attribute for the current element

- A string value that will be used as a value for the current element

- A null value that will be ignored

- An IEnumerable object that will be enumerated and its elements added recursively into the XML document

- A value (variable, constant, property, or method call) to be used as value for the current element

- An XComment object that will be added as child element

- An XProcessingInstruction object that will generate a processing instruction as a child element

Using the XDeclaration Class

You can use an XDocument object to specify the XML declaration, as in Listing 3-16.

Listing 3-16. Using the XDocument Class Constructor to Specify XML Declaration Attributes

```
XDocument xml = new XDocument(
    new XDeclaration("1.0", "UTF-8", "yes"),
    new XElement("people",
    new XElement("idperson",
    new XAttribute("id", 1),
    new XAttribute("year", 2004),
    new XAttribute("salaryyear", "10000,0000"))));

System.IO.StringWriter sw = new System.IO.StringWriter();
xml.Save(sw);
Console.WriteLine(sw);
```

Caution   There is a bug in the XDeclaration constructor. Even if you set the encoding value to a value other than UTF-16, UTF-16 will be used.

Listing 3-16 also shows using XAttribute to add attribute values to the current element. Moreover, the Save method, provided by both the XDocument and XElement classes, saves the complete XML document into a StringWriter object (see "Loading and Saving XML" later in this chapter). Figure 3-8 shows the output of Listing 3-16.

```
C:\WINDOWS\system32\cmd.exe                                    - □ ×
<?xml version="1.0" encoding="utf-16" standalone="yes"?>
<people>
  <idperson id="1" year="2004" salaryyear="10000,0000" />
</people>
Press any key to continue . . .
```

Using the XNamespace Class to Create an XML Document

If you need to use XML namespace declarations, use the XNamespace class.
Using it to create an XML document is similar to using it to query elements
and attributes. We have to use the namespace variable in the XElement class
constructor (or in the XAttribute class if we are going to specify an
attribute), and add the string that represents the name of the element or the
attribute.

Listing 3-17 shows how to produce the first three rows of the Hello_LINQ to
XML.xml Microsoft Word XML file used during previous examples.

*Listing 3-17. Reproducing an XML Document Snippet That Has
Microsoft Word Format*

```
XNamespace w =
    "http://schemas.microsoft.com/office/word/2003/wordml";

XDocument word = new XDocument(
    new XDeclaration("1.0","utf-8", "yes"),
    new XProcessingInstruction("mso-application",
                              "progid=\"Word.Document\""),
    new XElement(w + "wordDocument",
    new XAttribute(XNamespace.Xmlns + "w",
    w. NamespaceName)));

System.IO.StringWriter sw = new System.IO.StringWriter();
word.Save(sw);

Console.WriteLine(sw);
```

The bold code shows how to add a namespace and how to add an element and attribute associated with that namespace. The output of this code is as follows:

```
<?xml version="1.0" encoding="UTF-8" standalone="yes"?>
<?mso-application progid="Word.Document"?>
<w:wordDocument xmlns:w="http://schemas.microsoft.com/office/word/2003/wordml" />
```

Transforming XML

A really cool feature of the XElement class constructor is that it can take an IEnumerable<XElement> collection as an argument. The constructor will iterate automatically through the collection and create child elements of the current element.

This kind of collection is usually produced by a LINQ query, so we could query an XML document and produce a new XML document with different characteristics. This process is called *XML transformation*, and it's usually done with the W3C's XSL Transformations (XSLT) language.

However, by using functional construction and providing an IEnumerable collection to the XElement constructor we can easily transform an XML document using LINQ to XML.

In Listing 3-18 some information within the People XML document is transformed into an HTML table.

Listing 3-18. Transforming an XML Document into HTML Code

```
XElement xml = XElement.Load(@"..\..\People.xml");

XElement html = new XElement("HTML",
                new XElement("BODY",
                   new XElement("TABLE",
                     new XElement("TH", "ID"),
                     new XElement("TH", "Full Name"),
                     new XElement("TH", "Role"),
from p in xml.Descendants("person")
```

```
join r in xml.Descendants("role") on (int) p.Element("idrole")
equals (int) r.Element("id")
select new  XElement("TR",
        new XElement("TD", p.Element("id").Value),
        new XElement("TD", p.Element("firstname").Value
        + " " + p.Element("lastname").Value),
        new XElement("TD",
          r.Element("roledescription").Value)))));

html.Save(@"C:\People.html");
```

The bold code in Listing 3-18 is the LINQ to XML query used to create the HTML table content. It joins person information in the XML document with role information. Then it selects the values that correspond to the HTML columns declared in the HTML header. The output is then saved into an HTML page using the Save method (see Figure 3-9).

Figure 3-9. The People XML document transformed into HTML

Loading and Saving XML

LINQ to XML provides easy methods to load and save XML documents. We've already used Load and Save in some of the examples in this chapter. The Load method you've used accepts a string argument that specifies the path where the XML file is located. Similarly, the Save method accepts a string argument in which you specify the path to store the XML document. However, these methods have other interesting overloads that we we'll look at soon.

Also, some other methods deserve mention. For example, the Parse method provided by the XElement class allows developers to build an XML document starting from a string (see Listing 3-19).

Listing 3-19. Building an XML Document from a String

```
string doc = @"<people>
                <!-- Person section -->
                <person>
                    <id>1</id>
                    <firstname>Carl</firstname>
                    <lastname>Lewis</lastname>
                    <idrole>1</idrole>
                </person>
            </people>";
XElement xml = XElement.Parse(doc);
Console.WriteLine(xml);
```

If you uses the .NET XmlReader and XmlWriter classes to read and write XML documents, you can pass these objects to the Load and Save methods. Listing 3-20 shows how to use XmlReader and XmlWriter with Load() and Save().

Listing 3-20. Reading an XML Document with XmlReader and Saving It with XmlWriter

```
XmlReader reader = XmlReader.Create(@"..\..\People.xml");
XDocument xml = XDocument.Load(reader);
Console.WriteLine(xml);
```

```
XElement idperson = xml.Descendants("idperson").Last();
idperson.Add(new XElement("idperson",
                new XAttribute("id", 1),
                new XAttribute("year", 2006),
                new XAttribute("salaryyear", "160000,0000")));

StringWriter sw = new StringWriter();
XmlWriter w = XmlWriter.Create(sw);
xml.Save(w);
w.Close();
Console.WriteLine(sw.ToString());
```

The static **Create** method creates an **XmlReader** object and reads the XML document from the path specified as the argument:

```
XmlReader reader = XmlReader.Create(@"..\..\People.xml");
```

Then the **XDocument**'s **Load** method loads the **XmlReader** object, building the LINQ to XML document structure:

```
XDocument xml = XDocument.Load(reader);
```

Similarly, the static **Create** method creates an **XmlWriter** object based on a **StringWriter** object:

```
StringWriter sw = new StringWriter();
XmlWriter w = XmlWriter.Create(sw);
```

This is necessary when you want to write the XML output to a string. The **Save** method provided by the **XDocument** class (the same as for the **XElement** class) accepts the **XmlWriter** object and stores the changes to the XML document in the **StringWriter** object.

Figure 3-10 shows that a new **idperson** element has been added to the source XML document.

Figure 3-10. The salary element has a new idperson child

```
C:\WINDOWS\system32\cmd.exe                                          - □ ×
                <roledescription>Developer</roledescription>
        </role>
        <!-- Salary section -->
        <salary>
                <idperson id="1" year="2004" salaryyear="10000,0000" />
                <idperson id="1" year="2005" salaryyear="15000,0000"><idperson i
d="1" year="2006" salaryyear="160000,0000" /></idperson>
        </salary>
</people>

Press any key to continue . . . _
```

Listing 3-20 previewed the code to modify an XML document. In the next section you'll see how to modify XML documents with XElement methods.

Modifying XML

LINQ to XML provides all the methods needed to insert, modify, and delete elements in an existing XML document.

Inserting Elements in an XML Document

In the following code snippet (a duplicate of Listing 3-20) the code that adds a new element to the XML document appears in boldface:

```
XmlReader reader = XmlReader.Create(@"..\..\People.xml");
XDocument xml = XDocument.Load(reader);
Console.WriteLine(xml);

XElement idperson = xml.Descendants("idperson").Last();
idperson.Add(new XElement("idperson",
            new XAttribute("id", 1),
            new XAttribute("year", 2006),
            new XAttribute("salaryyear", "160000,0000")));

StringWriter sw = new StringWriter();
XmlWriter w = XmlWriter.Create(sw);
xml.Save(w);
w.Close();
Console.WriteLine(sw.ToString());
```

To add an element to a specific position in an XML document, we have to navigate to the desired node using the `Element` or `Descendants` methods. Then, using the `Add` method of `XElement`, we can add the element in the right place.

Note   If you use the `Add` method without establishing a specific XML document position, the new element will be added at the end of the document.

We can use the `AddFirst` method to insert a new element at the beginning of an XML document, just after the root element, as in Listing 3-21.

Listing 3-21. Using AddFirst to Insert a New Element at the Beginning of an XML Document

```
XElement xml = XElement.Load(@"..\..\People.xml");

xml.AddFirst(new XElement("person",
            new XElement("id",5),
            new XElement("firstname","Tom"),
            new XElement("lastname","Cruise"),
            new XElement("idrole",1)));
Console.WriteLine(xml);
```

Figure 3-11 shows the output for Listing 3-21.

Figure 3-11. Adding a new person element at the beginning of the XML document

```
C:\WINDOWS\system32\cmd.exe                              _ □ ×
<people>
  <person>
    <id>5</id>
    <firstname>Tom</firstname>
    <lastname>Cruise</lastname>
    <idrole>1</idrole>
  </person>
  <!-- Person section -->
  <person>
    <id>1</id>
    <firstname>Carl</firstname>
    <lastname>Lewis</lastname>
    <idrole>1</idrole>
  </person>
  <person>
    <id>2</id>
    <firstname>Tom</firstname>
```

Using the `AddAfterSelf` and `AddBeforeSelf` methods after positioning the cursor at the desired node, we can add a new element after or before the current node, respectively.

Updating Elements in an XML Document

Using the `SetElementValue` method of `XElement`, we can update an element with a new value. In Listing 3-22 we change the description of the first role contained in the People XML document.

Listing 3-22. Using the SetElementValue Method to Modify an Element's Value

```csharp
XElement xml = XElement.Load(@"..\..\People.xml");

XElement role = xml.Descendants("role").First();
Console.WriteLine("-=-=ORIGINAL-=-=");
Console.WriteLine(role);

role.SetElementValue("roledescription", "Actor");
Console.WriteLine(string.Empty);
Console.WriteLine("-=-=UPDATED-=-=");
Console.WriteLine(role);
```

After having reached the first `role` node, we can use the `SetElementValue` method to change the role description to the `Actor`. (Figure 3-12 shows the output.)

Figure 3-12. The SetElementValue method changes the value of an XML element.

```
C:\WINDOWS\system32\cmd.exe                                    - □ ×
-=-=ORIGINAL-=-=
<role>
   <id>1</id>
   <roledescription>Manager</roledescription>
</role>

-=-=UPDATED-=-=
<role>
   <id>1</id>
   <roledescription>Actor</roledescription>
</role>
Press any key to continue . . .
```

Similarly, using the `SetAttributeValue` method of the `XElement` class we can change the value of the specified attribute. (See Listing 3-23.)

Listing 3-23. Changing the Value of an Attribute by Using the SetAttributeValue Method

```
XElement xml = XElement.Load(@"..\..\People.xml");

XElement role = xml.Descendants("idperson").First();
Console.WriteLine("-=-=ORIGINAL-=-=");
Console.WriteLine(role);

role.SetAttributeValue("year", "2006");
Console.WriteLine(string.Empty);
Console.WriteLine("-=-=UPDATED-=-=");
Console.WriteLine(role);
```

As you can see from the output in Figure 3-13, the year of the first `idperson` element is changed from 2004 to 2006.

Figure 3-13. Just like the SetElementValue method changes an element's value by using the SetAttributeValue method, it can change an attribute's value

```
C:\WINDOWS\system32\cmd.exe                                      _ □ ×
-=-=ORIGINAL-=-=
<idperson id="1" year="2004" salaryyear="10000,0000" />

-=-=UPDATED-=-=
<idperson id="1" year="2006" salaryyear="10000,0000" />
Press any key to continue . . .
```

Note Using the SetElementValue and SetAttributeValue methods with elements and attributes not already present in an XML document is equivalent to adding them to the current element. On the other hand, specifying a null value with an existing element removes that element from the XML document.

Finally, to replace an entire section of the XML document with new values, use the ReplaceNodes method of XElement, as in Listing 3-24.

Listing 3-24. Replacing a Whole XML Document Section by Using the ReplaceNodes Method

```
XElement xml = XElement.Load(@"..\..\People.xml");

xml.Element("person").ReplaceNodes(new XElement("id", 5),
                               new XElement("firstname","Tom"),
                               new XElement("lastname","Cruise"),
                               new XElement("idrole",1));
Console.WriteLine(xml);
```

The first **person** element is substituted with a new person, as shown in Figure 3-14.

Figure 3-14. The output for Listing 3-24

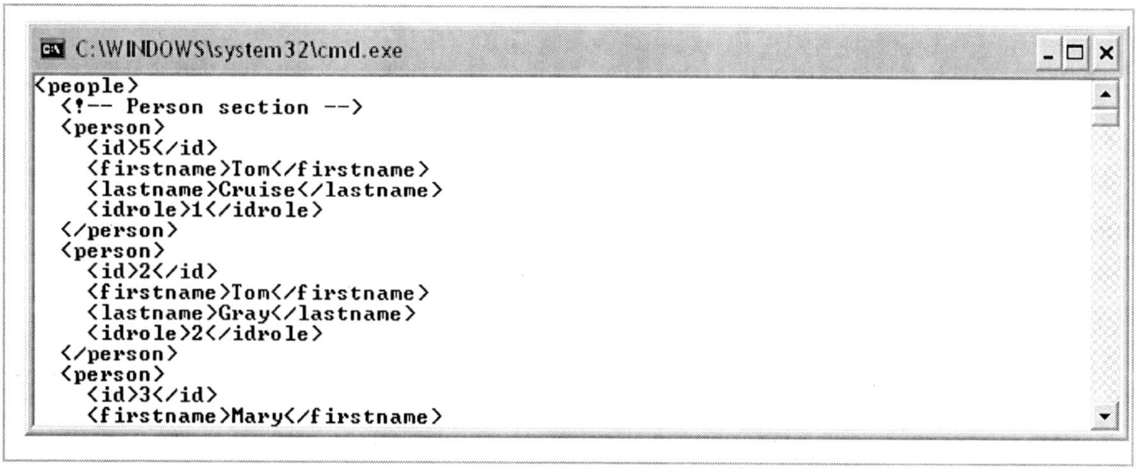

```
C:\WINDOWS\system32\cmd.exe                                    _ □ ×
<people>
  <!-- Person section -->
  <person>
    <id>5</id>
    <firstname>Tom</firstname>
    <lastname>Cruise</lastname>
    <idrole>1</idrole>
  </person>
  <person>
    <id>2</id>
    <firstname>Tom</firstname>
    <lastname>Gray</lastname>
    <idrole>2</idrole>
  </person>
  <person>
    <id>3</id>
    <firstname>Mary</firstname>
```

Deleting Elements from an XML Document

The XElement class provides two methods to remove an element from an XML document: Remove and Remove Content.

The Remove method applied to the current node removes that element from the XML document. Using the Remove method with an IEnumerable<XElement> collection iterates through all the elements and removes them (see Listing 3-25).

Listing 3-25. Removing an idperson Element and the role Section

```csharp
XElement xml = XElement.Load(@"..\..\People.xml");

xml.Descendants("idperson").First().Remove();

xml.Elements("role").Remove();

Console.WriteLine(xml);
```

Figure 3-15 shows the output of this code snippet.

```
C:\WINDOWS\system32\cmd.exe                                          _ □ ×
    <lastname>Ferracchiati</lastname>
    <idrole>1</idrole>
 </person>
 <!-- Role section -->
 <!-- Salary section -->
 <salary>
    <idperson id="1" year="2005" salaryyear="15000,0000" />
 </salary>
</people>
Press any key to continue . . . _
```

The second removal method that XElement provides is RemoveNodes, which lets you remove an entire section of an XML document. In Listing 3-26 all the content of the first role element is removed.

Listing 3-26. Removing the Content of the First role Element

```csharp
XElement xml = XElement.Load(@"..\..\People.xml");

xml.Element("role").RemoveNodes();

Console.WriteLine(xml);
```

As you can see from the output in Figure 3-16, the first role element loses its content and is replaced by an empty tag (<role />).

Figure 3-16. The RemoveNodes method applied to the first role element

```
 C:\WINDOWS\system32\cmd.exe                                    - □ ×
  </person>
  <!-- Role section -->
  <role />
  <role>
    <id>2</id>
    <roledescription>Developer</roledescription>
  </role>
  <!-- Salary section -->
  <salary>
    <idperson id="1" year="2004" salaryyear="10000,0000" />
    <idperson id="1" year="2005" salaryyear="15000,0000" />
  </salary>
</people>
Press any key to continue . . . _
```

RemoveAttribute() called on the current element removes all its attributes. To remove just a single attribute, you have to set that attribute's value to null using the SetAttributeValue method, as mentioned in the note after Listing 3-23.

LINQ to XML and LINQ to SQL

The final section of this chapter covers the integration aspects between two LINQ technologies: LINQ to XML and LINQ to SQL.

In Listing 3-27 we use a LINQ to SQL query to retrieve all the person rows from the database, which produces an XML file similar to the People.xml file.

Listing 3-27. Querying the SQL Server People Database to Produce an XML Document from a LINQ to SQL Query

```
PeopleDataContext people = new PeopleDataContext();

XElement xml = new XElement("people",
                    from p in people.People
                    select  new XElement("person",
                                new XElement("id", p.ID),
                                new XElement("firstname", p.FirstName),
```

```
                                    new XElement("lastname", p.LastName),
                                    new XElement("idrole", p.IDRole)));
        Console.WriteLine(xml);
```

Using a LINQ to SQL query as an argument to the XElement constructor, we
can produce an XML document in which content comes directly from
database data. Figure 3-17 shows the output of the code snippet in Listing
3-27.

*Figure 3-17. The XML document produced by querying the People
database*

```
C:\WINDOWS\system32\cmd.exe                                    _ □ ×
<people>
  <person>
    <id>1</id>
    <firstname>Carl</firstname>
    <lastname>Lewis</lastname>
    <idrole>1</idrole>
  </person>
  <person>
    <id>2</id>
    <firstname>Tom</firstname>
    <lastname>Gray</lastname>
    <idrole>2</idrole>
  </person>
  <person>
    <id>3</id>
    <firstname>Mary</firstname>
    <lastname>Grant</lastname>
    <idrole>2</idrole>
  </person>
  <person>
    <id>61</id>
    <firstname>Fabio</firstname>
    <lastname>Ferracchiati</lastname>
    <idrole>1</idrole>
  </person>
</people>
Press any key to continue . . .
```

Now consider taking an XML document as the data source and querying
the database to search for new rows. If the XML document contains new
rows not present in the database, the code in Listing 3-28 uses LINQ to
SQL to add them to the database.

Listing 3-28. Searching for New Records in an XML Document and Eventually Adding Them to the Database

```
xml.Add(new XElement("person",
            new XElement("id", 5),
            new XElement("firstname", "Tom"),
            new XElement("lastname", "Cruise"),
            new XElement("idrole", 1)));

Console.WriteLine(xml);

AddPerson(xml, people);
```

Using the XML document created in Listing 3-27, the code adds a new person element and passes the final XElement object to the AddPerson method that checks the XML document for new records, eventually adding them to the database. Listing 3-29 shows the code of the AddPerson method.

Listing 3-29. Adding a New Person Record, Read from the XML Document, That Is Not Already Present in the Database

```
private static void AddPerson(XElement xml, PeopleDataContext peopledb)
{
    var people = xml.Descendants("person");
    foreach(var person in people)
    {
        var query = from p in peopledb.People
                    where p.ID == (int)person.Element("id")
                    select p;

        if (query.ToList().Count == 0)
        {
            Person per = new Person();
            per.FirstName = person.Element("firstname").Value;
```

```
                    per.LastName = person.Element("lastname").Value;
                    per.IDRole = (int)person.Element("idrole");
                    peopledb.People.Add(per);
                }
            }

            peopledb.SubmitChanges();
        }
```

The body of the AddPerson method retrieves the collection of person elements in the XML document:

```
var people = xml.Descendants("person");
```

Then it iterates through the collection and queries the People table by primary key for each person:

```
var query = from p in peopledb.People
            where p.ID == (int)person.Element("id")
            select p;
```

If the collection produced by the ToList method doesn't contain items, then the person is not in the table; in that case, a new Person object is created, filled with values read from the XML document, and added to People.

Once all the XML elements have been processed, the insertions are propagated to the database with SubmitChanges().

Summary

You've seen that querying an XML document with LINQ to XML is easy and requires little more than knowledge of LINQ query syntax. You no longer have to be an expert in XML to handle XML data easily. You can focus on what you want to do rather than on how to do it!

Moreover, you've seen how LINQ to XML allows you to easily create XML documents and modify their contents.

We've reached the end of the chapter, as well as the end of the book. You've seen all the major features of a great new technology, LINQ, which shipped with the new .NET Framework 3.5 and its new version of the C# and VB languages. LINQ is the future of .NET data access—and the future is now.

Related Titles

Rattz, Joseph C. *Pro LINQ: Language Integrated Query in C# 2008*, Berkeley, CA: Apress, 2008

Mehta, Vijay P. *Pro LINQ: Object Relational Mapping in C# 2008*, Berkeley, CA: Apress, 2008

Joshi, Bipin. *Beginning XML with C# 2008: From Novice to Professional*, Berkeley, CA: Apress, 2008

Ferracchiati, Fabio. *Linq for VB 2005*, Berkeley, CA: Apress, 2007

Agarwal, Vidya Vrat, & Huddleston, James. *Beginning VB 2008 Databases: From Novice to Professional*, Berkeley, CA: Apress, 2008

Herman, Todd, et al. *Visual Basic 2008 Recipes: From Novice to Professional*, Berkeley, CA: Apress, 2008

Copyright

LINQ for Visual C# 2008

© 2008 by Fabio Claudio Ferracchiati

ISBN-13 (electronic): 978-1-4302-1581-3

ISBN-13 (paperback): 978-1-4302-1580-6

Trademarked names may appear in this book. Rather than use a trademark symbol with every occurrence of a trademarked name, we use the names only in an editorial fashion and to the benefit of the trademark owner, with no intention of infringement of the trademark.

Distributed to the book trade in the United States by Springer-Verlag New York, Inc., 233 Spring Street, 6th Floor, New York, NY 10013, and outside the United States by Springer-Verlag GmbH & Co. KG, Tiergartenstr. 17, 69112 Heidelberg, Germany.

In the United States: phone 1-800-SPRINGER, fax 201-348-4505, e-mail orders@springer-ny.com, or visit http://www.springer-ny.com. Outside the United States: fax +49 6221 345229, e-mail orders@springer.de, or visit http://www.springer.de.

For information on translations, please contact Apress directly at 2855 Telegraph Ave, Suite 600, Berkeley, CA 94705. Phone 510-549-5930, fax 510-549-5939, e-mail info@apress.com, or visit http://www.apress.com.